THE
GRACE
TO
GROW

THE GRACE TO GROW: THE POWER OF CHRISTIAN FAITH IN
EMOTIONAL HEALING

A Word Book / published by arrangement with
Bantam Books, Inc.

Copyright © 1984 by William P. Wilson and Kathryn Slattery
Printed in the United States of America

Though the case histories that appear in this book are used with permission,
names and certain identifying details have been changed.

Unless otherwise indicated, Scripture quotations are from the *Good News Bible*,
the Bible in Today's English Version, copyright © American Bible Society 1976.

Scripture quotations identified RSV are from the Revised Standard Version of the
Bible, copyright © 1946, 1952, © 1971 and 1973 by the Division of Christian
Education of the National Council of Churches of Christ in the U.S.A.

Library of Congress Cataloging in Publication Data

Wilson, William P., 1922–
    The grace to grow.

    1. Spiritual healing. 2. Emotions—Religious aspects
—Christianity. 3. Wilson, William P., 1922–
4. Psychotherapy. I. Slattery, Kathryn. II. Title.
BT732.5.W54   1984   261.5'15   84–2329
ISBN 0–8499–0395–5

William P. Wilson, M.D.

with Kathryn Slattery

THE GRACE TO GROW

The Power of Christian Faith in Emotional Healing

WORD BOOKS
PUBLISHER
WACO, TEXAS

A DIVISION OF
WORD, INCORPORATED

To my father
for
forty-four years of prayer

Contents

Preface

For years, psychiatry and Christianity have been pitted against each other as adversaries. At one end of the scale, fundamentalist believers have been known to distrust medical science in general, maintaining that faith in God is all a person needs to be healed. At the other end of the scale, nonbelieving scientists have put little stock in religion, maintaining that it represents little more than archaic, wishful thinking.

As a physician and scientist who also happens to be a Christian, it is my belief that far from being detrimental, religion can, in fact, be beneficial to mental health. No longer is there justification for any sense of conflict or schism between religion and medicine—particularly psychiatry. Rather, Christianity and psychiatry can, with great effectiveness, work together to mend broken lives. In my more than thirty-five years of practice, teaching, and research, I've witnessed too many healings and accumulated too much evidence to conclude otherwise.

It is one of humankind's greatest misfortunes that over the years modern medicine has so willfully divorced itself from its theologically rooted origins. In contrast to the treatment of the more easily understood body and mind, treatment of the *whole person*—including the human *spirit*—has been overlooked, ignored, and denied. In his book, *Miracles*, C. S. Lewis speaks of this unfortunate schism between religion and science in this way:

And since the Sixteenth Century, when Science was born, the minds of men have been increasingly turned outward to know Nature and to master her. They have been increasingly engaged in those specialised inquiries for which truncated thought is the correct method. It is therefore not in the least astonishing that they should have forgotten the evidence of the Supernatural. The deeply ingrained habit of truncated thought—what we call "scientific" habit of mind—was indeed certain to lead to Naturalism, unless this tendency was continually corrected from some other source. But no other source was at hand, for during the same period men of science were coming to be metaphysically and theologically uneducated.*

In this age of vast scientific and technological advances, many of the ideas proposed in this book may seem to some to be disconcertingly transcendent. But such must be, in light of the fact that my purpose for writing this book is this: to demonstrate, through my personal story and through the dramatic case histories of others, that our God is a loving God who passionately desires health and wholeness for His people. Through the Holy Spirit, the living Jesus Christ, He continues to transform lives and work wondrous healings in much the same manner as He did when He walked the earth nearly two-thousand years ago—sometimes intervening in a person's life miraculously, more often employing the skills and talents of willing servants like myself and others.

It is my fondest hope that through this book you will not only experience the wonder and healing power of Christ's love in your own life—but that you will, in turn, be given the power to reach out and extend that love to others.

WILLIAM P. WILSON, M.D.

---

* C. S. Lewis, *Miracles* (copyright 1947 by Macmillan Publishing Co., Inc., New York, and William Collins Sons & Co. Ltd., London; renewed 1975 by Arthur Owen Barfield and Alfred Cecil Harwood). Used by permission.

PART I

MY
STORY

God's Grace Revealed

1

With No Worlds Left
to Conquer

"Hey, Bill. Got a minute?"

I looked up from my desk to see an old colleague and dear friend standing in the doorway of my office at Duke University's Medical Center. He was an internist—one of the best in the country. I was a psychiatrist.

"Sure," I said, pushing aside the patient reports I'd been working on. "Come on in."

It was February, 1964, and as was usual for me, I'd been working late. Glancing at my watch, I noticed that it was nearly eight o'clock. The cold fluorescent lighting cast thin blue shadows across my friend's usually warm and animated features. He appeared tired. Sighing wearily, he sat down in the chair facing me.

"What's up?" I asked.

"Well," he responded, with a tight little smile, "you may find this hard to understand, but lately it seems that my life is a drag." He shook his head. "I just don't understand it. I mean, you'd think that I had everything in this world a person could want. Like you, I've recently been appointed as a full professor here at the University—not bad for a guy barely in his forties. And like you, I've got unlimited access to a huge laboratory, the best of research facilities, and a fabulous library. Esteemed journals publish my papers. The government awards me grants. I've got a great wife and nice kids. So why," he leaned back in his chair and regarded me with a wry smile, "do I feel so darn empty inside?"

For a moment I could think of nothing to say. Clearly my friend's complaint—a feeling of emptiness—was not indicative of any serious mental illness. Didn't everyone feel that way at times? I know I did.

Suddenly, a verse from Samuel Butler's seventeenth-century classic poem, *Hudibras*, came to mind:

> The whole world was not half so wide
> To Alexander when he cry'd
> Because he had but one to subdue. . . .

The lines referred to Alexander III, of Macedon, the great world conqueror of ancient times.

"Say," I remarked, "I know what your problem is. You've got Alexander the Great's Syndrome!"

"What?"

"You're like Alexander the Great," I repeated. "As legend has it, with no more worlds left to conquer, Alexander sat down and wept. Doesn't that describe how you're feeling?"

"Why yes," replied my friend, rather pleased at the comparison. "I believe you're right. Alexander the Great's Syndrome. Hey, I kind of like that."

For the next several minutes the two of us discussed possible reasons for my friend's sense of emptiness and searched for ways through which he might remedy the situation. We realized that in the existing medical literature there was no specific name for my friend's malady; within philosophy and the arts, however, it was commonly known as existential despair—that profoundly disturbing sense that one's life has no meaning, that there is no purpose for one's existence.

While our discussion was certainly provocative, we were unable to arrive at any guaranteed cure for my friend's problem. I wished that I could give him an answer that would offer real help. But all I could say was, "The way you're feeling isn't unusual. If it's any consolation, I often feel the same way."

My friend grinned ruefully.

"Try not to let it get you down," I advised.

"All right," he agreed, rising from his chair to go. "I guess you're right."

The interlude left me feeling vaguely depressed. *Why,* I wondered, *did I feel like my friend more often than I cared to admit?*

That night, I lay awake in bed unable to sleep. I couldn't stop thinking about the conversation I had had with my friend, and how his life, in spite of all his worldly success, had no meaning.

The more I thought about it, the more worthy the subject seemed of receiving some sort of commentary in the medical literature; in a matter of minutes I decided that I would write an article on the subject. Sitting up and turning on the bedside lamp, I reached for the pad and pencil on my bedstand and began jotting down a few notes. I'd been working like this for about five minutes, when I felt the gentle touch of my wife, Elizabeth's hand on my forearm.

"Honey?" she inquired softly. "You still up?"

"Damn it, Elizabeth!" I snapped. "Can't you see I'm busy?"

The moment the words escaped my lips, I was filled with remorse. I'd always had a nasty temper, and I could turn the air blue with cursing when I had a mind to. Because of these traits I had earned the reputation of being a holy terror among my interns and resident doctors at the hospital. Lately it seemed that both my bad language and hot temper were getting worse. Just the other day, while annoyed at the sloppy job that had been done by lab technicians in taking an electroencephalograph reading (an electroencephalograph is an instrument used to record electrical activity in the brain), I had grabbed the offending charts—some forty feet of fan-folded paper—and hurled them across the lab where they crashed into the window at the far end of the room, knocked down the venetian blinds, and sent terrified technicians scurrying for cover. Then, too, I had been filled with embarrassment and remorse for my behavior.

"I'm sorry," I apologized to Elizabeth.

"That's all right," she replied. By now she was used to my outbursts. Sitting up, she peered over my shoulder at my notes. "You working on a new article?"

"Yep."

"You want to tell me about it?"

I put down my pencil.

"A good friend was in my office this evening," I said. "He was feeling kind of low. Downright depressed. He told me he was tired of living. He felt his life had no meaning."

"That's a shame," said Elizabeth.

"Yes," I agreed. "But it's not the first time I've heard such a complaint. I'd like to look into the subject of existential despair more deeply. I plan to write an article about people who, in the midst of success, suffer like my friend. Elizabeth . . ." Peering over my glasses, I regarded her intently. "Do you ever feel that life has no meaning?"

She shook her head.

"No," she replied. "You may think what I'm going to say is silly, Bill, but ever since I was a little girl and first believed in God, I've always sensed deep down inside that there is a reason for everything that happens to us in life— even bad things—and that everything will turn out for the best in the end."

"I don't think that's silly," I replied. "I think it's nice that your faith means so much to you. The trouble is, religion isn't scientific. Religion can't be proved. Religion can't be used to help a sick person get well. Aw, hell," I felt myself growing angry. "How'd we ever get on this subject anyhow?"

"Your article," she reminded me softly. "You were telling me about your article. It sounds to me like a very interesting subject, Bill. I know you'll do a good job." She kissed me lightly on the cheek. "Please don't stay up too late now, will you? You really do need your sleep."

But already lost in thought, busy jotting down more notes, I didn't answer.

In following weeks, I began researching my paper on existential despair, spending endless hours in the library searching the existing medical literature for any mention of such an affliction—but coming up with next to nothing. When I questioned several of my colleagues on the subject, however, a surprising number admitted that they suffered symptoms similar to those expressed by my friend.

Nearly a year later, in January, 1965, my finished article, which I had titled "Alexander's (The Great) Syndrome," was published in *Clinical Research*, one of medicine's better known professional journals. In the weeks following its publication, I was amazed to receive a deluge of mail from physicians all over the country, many confessing that they suffered from Alexander's Syndrome, and thanking me profusely for writing the article.

Several months later, when the *British Medical Journal* published an editorial commentary about my article, I once again received a flood of letters—this time from doctors all over the world.

Still, it wasn't until one balmy spring evening in 1965, as I was sitting at the kitchen table sharing a few of these letters with Elizabeth, that it suddenly occurred to me that I too, provided no less than a classic case of someone afflicted with Alexander's Syndrome!

Why, I wondered, *had it taken me so long to come to this realization? After all, wasn't it obvious that I had all the symptoms?*

Here I was at age forty-four, a full professor of psychiatry at one of America's finest universities. I had a bibliography that rivaled anyone in my field. I was an active officer in both state and regional professional societies. I was happily married, had five lovely children, and a host of friends. Yet, in a most disturbing way, my life was essentially meaningless. Daily I woke with a desperate need to keep on discovering new challenges, new goals to work toward—anything to provide my life with some sense of meaning.

With no worlds left to conquer, what more was there for me to do?

2

Dropped in a Bucket of Love

It was early summer, 1965. In my desperate quest to fill my life with activities and projects that would hopefully provide me with a sense of purpose, I had recently agreed to serve as a leader for my oldest son's Scout troop.

In two weeks, I would be joining my son Bill and his friends on an eight-day Scouting trip deep in the wilds of northern Minnesota's Quetico-Superior Wilderness Area. The trip, a canoe expedition, would take us above the Canadian border via a 169-mile circular route, culminating with a twenty-four-hour nonstop "survival paddle." For this reason, I had recently initiated a self-prescribed emergency program of jogging and sit-ups to get in shape.

"You know, Dad," commented Bill during one of my workouts, "I think you're looking forward to this trip as much as I am."

He was right.

As a boy, I'd spent much of my childhood hunting, fishing and exploring the wonders of North Carolina's woods. I'd never been a religious person, but there was something about those quiet times in the forest that had been—well—special.

Yes, I was looking forward to the trip. The change, I hoped, would do me good.

The moment I shook hands with our expedition leader, Ray Mattson, I liked him. A tall, lean-muscled college student with copper-colored hair and beard, he looked from head to toe like a contemporary of Lewis and Clark. His hair was held back from his handsome face by a rolled bandanna; he wore a forest green shirt and pants tied at the waist with a hand-woven sash. At six-feet, six-inches, Ray was the kind of guy who could pick up a hundred-pound canoe and thirty-five-pound backpack, and jog for five miles without stopping.

With unflagging enthusiasm, Ray led us on an unforgettable journey that challenged the strength and skills of the hardiest troop member. Just as I had hoped, it was glorious to be out in the fresh air, to hear the whisper of the windswept pines, to gaze up at night to the starry sky—the confusion of stars like so many millions of diamonds spilled upon a velvet canopy.

The seventh day of our expedition fell on a Sunday. That morning, according to Scout rules, Ray gathered us together for a brief worship service. Standing atop a craggy boulder, he gave a little talk based upon the twenty-third chapter of the book of Matthew in the Bible.

"'Blind Pharisee!' he recalled the words of Jesus. 'Clean what is inside the cup first, and then the outside will be clean too!'" (Matt. 23:26).

He went on to compare the wilderness, in all its splendor and untouched beauty, to the way the inside of our lives should be. Then he led us in a sing-a-long of simple religious songs that rang out pure and clear in the cool morning air. Listening to that sound, I felt something—some untapped emotion—stir deep inside of me.

It had been a long time, I realized, *since I had thought about God.*

That evening, as the sun was setting, I decided to walk to the edge of Basswood Lake, immense and sparkling beneath a pastel-painted sky. In a short while we would be embarking on the last leg of our survival paddle, an all-night journey. Then we would be heading home.

Spotting a sturdy log about thirty yards away, I walked over to it and sat down. Kicking off my moccasins, I let my bare feet play with the pebbly soil of the lake shore. My thoughts wandered back to the morning worship service and the strange effect it had had on me. As a man of science in a field where religion was often viewed with skepticism, the idea of a living God had always seemed remote and archaic. But there was nothing outdated about the morning's message—God wanted us clean and healthy, *inside* as well as out, in order to be the kind of human beings He had designed us to be. Inherent in that concept, pure and simple, was the essence of modern psychiatry.

Ruefully, I recalled the emptiness and lack of purpose I often felt. I also thought about my nasty temper and the way it often caused me to hurt the ones I loved most.

What was it, I wondered, *that could possibly clean up the inside of my life?*

It suddenly became clear to me that the only true way for me to clean up my life and be completely fulfilled wasn't through science—through medicine or psychiatry. It was through God. Looking out over the placid waters of Basswood Lake, I knew this was what I needed and wanted more than anything in the world—for God to come into my life and make me whole.

Before I knew it, tears were streaming down my face. As the sunset I had been watching melted into a golden blur, I felt as though I'd been dropped in a bucket of love. It was a feeling of love—of *being loved*—unlike anything I'd ever known. It bathed the deepest recesses of my soul, washing away all loneliness, despair, guilt, and anger. As I basked, dumbfounded, in the experience, an awesome thing began to happen. Gradually, I became aware of a Presence. Someone was with me!

This Someone, I perceived, was not only responsible for all the love I had been experiencing—He was the incarnation of Love Himself. It was then that I knew I was in the presence of God. He was real. He was truly with me.

Why is this happening to me? I thought. *I'm nobody special. God's got no reason to waste His time on me. Surely He's made some mistake.*

But God didn't leave me. As if in response to my doubts, He allowed His love to well up within me even stronger. I savored the experience as long as I could, but soon it was time to go.

That night, as we paddled in the moonlit darkness, I remained silent, lost in thought about what had happened at Basswood Lake. I looked over at the canoe on our port side and for a brief moment saw its bow and stern suspended on two waves. Moonlight flashed in the water beneath it, and the wet paddles glistened as if they had been dipped in mercury. It was incredibly beautiful.

Though I couldn't say exactly how, I knew that I had been changed. Everything seemed so clean, so bright, so new. Never had I felt so peaceful. And for the first time in many years I felt as though my life had purpose and meaning—I felt a sense of keen anticipation for what the future might hold.

When I returned home, I didn't tell anyone about my experience at Basswood Lake—not even Elizabeth. It was as though my relationship with God was too new, too fragile, to share. At the same time, I knew that what had happened to me was so real and concrete that I would defend it to the death. This, I think, is what frightened me the most. *Who would believe me? How could I ever prove what had happened?*

But over the next few days, there were noticeable changes in me. While it couldn't be said that my temper was any better, on several occasions I caught myself on the verge of swearing, only to find that I was literally unable to do so. My desire to curse had vanished. Understanding the deeply ingrained nature of this old habit of mine, and knowing as a psychiatrist how difficult such patterns of behavior are to break, I found the whole thing fascinating. And though I still didn't fully understand what had happened to me at Basswood Lake, I interpreted the rehabilitation of my mouth as being a kind of affirmation of the event. It also seemed that I loved my wife more, and I was more tolerant with the kids. If only through these small examples, I felt I now had proof, in ways more tangible than mere feelings, that I had changed.

Still, I told no one what had taken place. I returned to work and—as usual—threw myself into my teaching, patients, research, and writing. A few weeks after having been caught up in the old familiar routine, I began to wonder if what had happened to me at Basswood Lake might have been a dream.

One night, while going over a chapter on love that I had prepared months earlier for a book I was writing about human emotions, I was taken aback by how seriously lacking it was in depth and insight. *Why,* I wondered, *hadn't I noticed this before?*

It occurred to me that religious literature might help me learn more about love. Intrigued, I visited the university library, and checked out William James's classic, *The Varieties of Religious Experience.*

From the start, I found the book fascinating, and quickly became engrossed in James's discussion of the emotion of love in religious experiences. To illustrate his point, James describes in detail the conversion experiences of several individuals. One story in particular seemed remarkably familiar to me. It was this testimony of a young man who had been hiking for days in the Swiss Alps:

> I was in perfect health: we were on our sixth day of tramping, and in good training. . . . I felt neither fatigue, hunger, nor thirst, and my state of mind was equally healthy. . . . I was subject to no anxiety, either near or remote, for we had a good guide, and there was not a shadow of uncertainty about the road we should follow. I can best describe the condition in which I was by calling it a state of equilibrium. When all at once I experienced a feeling of being raised above myself, I felt the presence of God—I tell of the thing just as I was conscious of it—as if his goodness and his power were penetrating me altogether. The throb of emotion was so violent that I could barely tell the boys to pass on and not wait for me. I then sat

down on a stone, unable to stand any longer, and my eyes overflowed with tears. . . . Then, slowly, the ecstasy left my heart; that is, I felt that God had withdrawn the communion which he had granted, and I was able to walk on, but very slowly, so strongly was I still possessed by the interior emotion. Besides, I had wept uninterruptedly for several minutes, my eyes were swollen, and I did not wish my companions to see me. The state of ecstasy may have lasted four or five minutes, although it seemed at the time to last much longer. . . . The impression had been so profound that in climbing slowly the slope I asked myself if it were possible that Moses on Sinai could have had a more intimate communication with God. I think it well to add that in this ecstasy of mine God had neither form, color, odor, nor taste; moreover, that the feeling of his presence was accompanied with no determinate localization. It was rather as if my personality had been transformed by the presence of a *spiritual spirit*. But the more I seek words to express this intimate intercourse, the more I feel the impossibility of describing the thing by any of the usual images. At bottom the expression most apt to render what I felt is this: God was present, though invisible; he fell under no one of my senses, yet my consciousness perceived him. . . .

Suddenly this incredible realization exploded in my head: *I'm like that man! I've been converted!*

For a split second I was ecstatic with this discovery. But then, just as quickly, I was aghast.

No! I protested. *I can't have been converted! What will people think? They'll reject me. They'll think I'm crazy. I'd better not tell anyone. Maybe it really didn't happen, anyhow. Maybe it was just a hysterical response to exhaustion and stress. Maybe I'd better just forget about the whole thing.*

But as I read and reread the account of the young man in the Swiss Alps, I knew that I couldn't deny what had happened to me at Basswood Lake. To admit to my experience hurt my pride. It didn't correspond with the image I had of myself as a rational, intelligent and educated person. Moreover, to be "converted" was, as far as I could see, diametrically opposed to my identity as a psychiatrist.

Throughout my education and career, most of my teachers and colleagues had been opposed to religion in any form. Indeed, one of my professors became violently antagonistic if the subject was so much as raised in his presence. In both undergraduate and medical school, I had been taught that religious beliefs were mythological fabrications of man. Truth was to be found in the teachings of Sigmund Freud, of B. F. Skinner, in the scientific method. After all, wasn't every psychiatrist familiar with at least one deranged character who considered himself a modern-day prophet? Hadn't every psychiatrist treated patients—pathetic cases—who suffered needlessly under self-imposed burdens of guilt or hate that they insisted on justifying by Scripture? Didn't my own hospital, in fact, have a rule that prevented incoming patients from having Bibles?

Me, Bill Wilson, *converted?*

It just didn't seem possible.

3

The Beginnings of Change

One Saturday evening, a few weeks following my return from Minnesota, Elizabeth and I were enjoying a quiet evening at home. The kids had all gone to bed, and the two of us were curled up at either end of the family room sofa, each absorbed in a book.

Elizabeth, that is, was absorbed. I'd been unable to concentrate on anything for the past few days because of a question that had been nagging me. It was such a trivial issue, really. Finally, I decided to get it off my chest.

"Elizabeth, don't you think it would be nice if we took the kids to church tomorrow?"

Looking up from her book, she arched an eyebrow and regarded me quizzically. "Church? But Bill, you haven't stepped inside a church for twenty years. What's the occasion?"

"Uh, no occasion," I stammered. "I mean, I think it might set a good example—you know, for the kids." I still hadn't told Elizabeth about my experience at Basswood Lake, and the last thing in the world I wanted was for her to suspect that it was really *I* who wanted to attend church.

"Honestly," said Elizabeth, "you never fail to surprise me." She smiled. "But I think it's a wonderful idea. I think the kids will like it, too."

Elizabeth was not exaggerating when she said that I hadn't been inside a church for twenty years. By the time

27

Sundays rolled around I preferred to sleep in, go boating, fish, garden, putter around the yard—anything to avoid going to church. Since Basswood Lake, however, I'd found myself not only wanting to attend Sunday services but, for some hard to explain reason, needing to.

According to William James, I had been "converted." Though the word still made me wince, I did seem to possess most of the standard effects of conversion, such as:

- Loss of worry.

- Perception of spiritual truths that I'd previously been unable to grasp.

- Seeing the world as changed; experiencing a sense of newness and cleanliness, within and without.

- Development of a positive mood and sense of well-being; a mood consisting predominantly of the emotion of love, but also punctuated by feelings of awe and joy.

Still, the notion that I had been converted left me vaguely puzzled. *Converted to what?* I kept asking myself. While I may have stopped cursing, my temper was still as volatile as ever. All I knew for certain was that at Basswood Lake I had encountered God and experienced His love and power in a very real and personal way. To want to go to church, therefore, seemed an entirely appropriate response.

The next morning found the seven of us filling a pew at Durham's Asbury United Methodist Church. Many heads turned to greet us, and Elizabeth and the kids seemed especially happy to be there.

In many ways the church service had changed little from what I recalled as a younger man. The organist still played the same familiar preludes. The opening prayers and liturgy hadn't changed a bit. It didn't take too many Sundays for me to realize, however, that while church may not have changed very much, I most definitely had!

Every time we sang a hymn that told of God's greatness

or holiness—or of Jesus' love—I was amazed to find tears running down my face. Sometimes it was downright embarrassing. Even more curious was the fact that when the collection plate was passed, I actually wanted to give money! Not just whatever loose bills I happened to have, but personal checks for hefty amounts. Such things had never happened to me in the past, and I didn't know quite what to make of them.

Most unusual of all was my growing desire to read the Bible. One night, unable to resist the urge any longer, I dug out my only copy—a dusty, black leather-bound King James version that I had received as a young man. Opening the book eagerly, I was dismayed to discover that the Old English dialect of the text was nearly impossible for me to understand. In passing weeks, I continued to struggle to read my Bible, but with little success; the archaic language proved to be too formidable a barrier.

Nearly a year passed, and I failed to notice any more significant changes in my life as a result of my conversion. Then, in 1967, a new movement called "Lay Witness Missions" was introduced in the United Methodist Church. The purpose of the Missions was to share the reality of God's love with other Methodist congregations across the country through traveling teams of lay people.

One Sunday morning, several weeks before a Lay Witness team was to visit our church for our first Mission, our minister announced that several openings remained in the twenty-four-hour "prayer vigil" that was to precede the team's arrival. I'd never heard of a prayer vigil before, let alone participated in such a pious-sounding event. That's why I was surprised when I heard a small voice in my head urge, "Sign up! Sign up!"

Naw, I resisted. *That kind of stuff is for religious types.*

But the voice was persistent, and after the service I found myself standing in the church foyer, peering through my glasses at the prayer vigil sign-up list.

There were only two fifteen-minute time slots remaining; both were for early Friday morning at 2:15 and 2:30.

Still not fully understanding why, I penciled in my name beside the 2:15 A.M. opening.

On the evening of the vigil I went to bed early and set my alarm. At 1:45 A.M., I woke, dressed, splashed cold water on my face, and left for the church. I arrived on time, and entered the sanctuary. Kneeling at the communion rail I closed my eyes—when suddenly it occurred to me that I had no idea what to pray for. For a few moments I reflected on this fact and then said out loud, "Lord, I don't know what it is that this Lay Witness Mission team needs, but whatever it is, let them have it."

For the remaining fourteen minutes and some thirty-odd seconds, I knelt there, bewildered, struck with the realization that not only did I have no idea how to pray for the visiting Mission team; I didn't have the foggiest notion how to pray, period.

"Lord," I murmured hastily, upon hearing the sound of my replacement's approaching footsteps, "help me understand what it means to pray. Teach me how to do it!"

4

So Many Questions

The spring of 1968 was a season of unprecedented uneasiness and strife. On many university campuses across the nation students were demonstrating—and Duke was no exception. Some of the students were getting hurt in minor skirmishes.

Inevitably, one cloudy Friday afternoon in May, a major riot took place during which more than one-hundred students stormed and occupied the Administration Building. Ominous rumors of more impending violence circulated through the hospital. I left my office upset and shaken.

Safely home, I tried to unwind from the day's events by playing with the kids, working on a paper, taking a long, hot bath—nothing worked. Finally, exhausted, I crawled into bed—but even then I was unable to relax.

With nightmarish clarity, images of suffering, death, and despair—those darker sides of humankind's nature and existence which I preferred to deny or ignore—crowded my mind. . . .

As a young boy growing up in Fayetteville, North Carolina—a city infamous for its gambling, prostitution, and drug trafficking—I had been exposed to the seamier side of life through my after-school paper route which included a good part of the town's red-light district. I recalled the hardened faces of aging madams as they picked out coins from their beaded purses and, with scarlet-lacquered fingernails, pressed them into my palm. Often, on my way home, I pedaled my bicycle past run-down beer joints where dope dealers conducted their business in smoky back rooms. It was then that I began to realize that not everyone spent their nights snug beneath warm quilts, and woke each morning to breakfasts of steaming oatmeal and fresh-squeezed orange juice.

In 1947, I was graduated from Duke University's School of Medicine. The following year, working as an intern in the Panama Canal Zone at Ancon's Gorgas Hospital, I continued to be confronted with suffering and despair.

My first assignment was in the hospital's isolation unit. Polio was rampant at the time, and patients in all stages of the disease were pouring in.

A few nights after my arrival, I was on call for the emergency room when I admitted a lovely eighteen-year-old girl named Catarina, who was complaining of pain in her right foot. I immediately suspected polio, and my diagnosis was confirmed following an examination of a sample of her spinal fluid. The girl's dark brown eyes grew wide with terror as I told her the news. There was no treatment for polio in those days; all we could do as doctors was watch—and wait.

Over the next four days, Catarina developed an ascending paralysis of her right leg, then both legs, then her abdomen, her chest, and finally—what we had been dreading—her diaphragm. We were then forced to place Catarina in an iron lung. Two days later, all of Catarina's muscles were paralyzed. In two more days she died. I was by Catarina's side when her heart stopped, and as I felt the last beat, my own heart cried out, *Why? Why does she have to die? She had so much life left to live. So much love to give.*

There was no answer.

Frequently, another doctor and I would travel by cayuco (a mahogany dugout canoe) deep into the Canal Zone jungle to bring medicine and treatment to the native villagers.

Helpless victims of poverty and poor sanitation, the natives were so infested by intestinal parasites they did not possess the energy to work.

It was the children, however, who suffered the most. Though food was plentiful, three out of every five born in the dirt-floor, palm-thatched hovels died before reaching five years of age. One day, after holding one of these poor dead children in my arms and looking into the despairing eyes of the stricken parents, I began to ask myself some serious questions.

What about death? Is there an afterlife? If there is no afterlife, what possible words of consolation can I offer a grief-stricken survivor?

So many questions—yet I had no answers.

Ironically, my most significant encounter with suffering and despair was not to take place in the jungles of Panama, but much closer to home—at North Carolina's Dorothea Dix State Hospital in Raleigh.

Upon returning home after my year as an intern in Ancon, I was still undecided as to what area in medicine I wanted to specialize. For this reason, I was also without a residency. It was one of my psychiatry professors at Duke, Dr. Leslie Hohman, who suggested that I try working for one year at the State Hospital where there was a job opening in the psychiatric service. With some uncertainty (in those days, psychiatric medicine was still in its infancy and state hospitals were notorious for their poor working conditions) I took Dr. Hohman's advice.

At that time, Dorothea Dix State Hospital was a massive white-stuccoed, vermin-infested complex, dating back to post–Civil War days. While some of the buildings were newer, all were in poor repair. Only five physicians cared for 2,300 patients. There were few nurses or aides, and little modern medical equipment. In my new position, I was responsible for 500 chronically mentally ill patients, plus major administrative duties.

What bothered me even more than the hospital's deplorable working conditions and my heavy workload was the overwhelming hopelessness I felt for the fate of most of my patients. Because we were so severely understaffed there was not enough time to conduct individual psychotherapy with each patient, and because we had no money, we could not hire others to help us. Our basic therapeutic tools consisted of only the crudest drugs (effective pharmaceuticals for drug therapy as we know today had not yet been developed), and electric-shock therapy.

The longer I worked at Dorothea Dix, the more angry and frustrated I became. *Why was it,* I wondered, *that no one seemed to care about the mentally ill?* From my experience, it was clear that the state didn't care. Nor did the public. Nor, most sadly, did the medical profession.

Wanting to do something to help these forgotten and abandoned people—wanting to save them from being left to deteriorate in institutions like the one in which I was working—I decided that I would become a psychiatrist. As a psychiatrist, I looked forward to helping the mentally ill—not only by working with individuals on a one-to-one counseling basis, but also by doing research. It was my deepest hope that in some small way I might be able to alleviate the pain and suffering that seemed to be such a large part of the human condition. . . .

Looking back on my years in the Panama Canal Zone and at Dorothea Dix State Hospital—and now recalling the well-to-do students who were rioting at our university—I grew angry. How else was I to respond to affluent kids who feigned poverty in prefaded jeans and tattered tee-shirts, and who drove to antiestablishment rallies and campus seiges in expensive cars? When tired of rioting, they would retreat to the local bars to quaff a few brews, or perhaps head back to the dorms to smoke a few joints. The whole scenario just didn't seem fair.

Moreover, it didn't make sense. The world, it seemed, had turned upside down. Traditional value systems that had once formed the bedrock of our society were now crumbling. Still, I sensed that my students—with their desperate search for something to believe in—were in some ways more lost and deprived than the children I had treated in the Canal Zone. With this realization, my anger dissolved. In its place I felt an overwhelming sense of helplessness—much as I had felt for my patients when I was a young doctor at Dorothea Dix Hospital.

I loved my students. As a professor, it bothered me terribly that I had nothing of lasting value to offer them.

Mulling the whole confusing and distressing situation over in my mind, I suddenly felt a strong desire to pray. I'd never experienced such a powerful urge before—but I didn't question it.

"Lord," I prayed out loud, "I know I've never done anything to make this world a better place—but if You want me to, I'll go where You tell me to go, and do what You tell me to do. Help me to understand You better, Lord. Help me to understand what it is You want me to do with my life."

God didn't say anything back to me. But I did feel strangely peaceful. Listening to the sound of Elizabeth's soft breathing next to me, I felt my anxiety melt away. Turning over, I fell asleep.

5

Welcome to the Kingdom

Three days later, on a Monday evening, I was sitting in our church parlor attending a board meeting. I'd been a board member for several months now, and on this particular evening it was announced that Jim Patrick, a man I knew only slightly, had recently been elected as the North Carolina Conference Lay Leader. In this new position, Jim would be largely responsible for lay leadership in the area, including coordinating several Lay Witness Missions.

When the meeting had adjourned, I approached Jim and congratulated him on his election.

"If there's anything I can do to be of help," I shook his hand, "just let me know."

"Well thanks, Bill!" he replied. "As a matter of fact, there is something you can do. Three weeks from now, a team of us is heading down to Manteo to conduct a Lay Witness Mission. We'll be spending the weekend with a small church there, and would like it very much if you could join us."

"Gosh, Jim," I stammered—never dreaming that he would take me up on my offer—"thanks for thinking of me, but . . ."

I was about to decline, when I recalled my prayer of three nights earlier; my promise to God that I would go where He told me to go, and do what He told me to do. *But this?* I questioned. *A weekend away from home in the company of strangers?* Still, I couldn't shake the strong im-

pression that this was, indeed, exactly what God wanted
me to do.

"Sure I'll go," I heard myself saying. "But I think you
should know that I've never been on one of these things
before. I'm not sure what use I'll be to you."

"Don't you worry about that," grinned Jim. "We'll take
good care of you."

The small village of Manteo is located on what is known
as the Outer Banks of North Carolina—a rugged arrow of
coastline that juts eastward into the Atlantic and bears the
brunt of harsh nor'easters and late summer hurricanes. For
the most part, the inhabitants of Manteo make their living
from the sea and land as fishermen and farmers. Of English
descent, many of the villagers continue to speak in a curious dialect that retains some of its original Elizabethan
flavor. The people of Manteo are simple, hard-working
folk. When compared to the city sophisticates of a college
town like Durham—just a few hundred miles away—they
seemed to me to be an anachronism. As I made prepara-
tions for the trip, I found myself wondering what we could
possibly have in common.

It was a warm Friday evening in May when our Lay
Witness Mission team pulled into the parking lot at Manteo's Methodist Church. A crowd was waiting to greet us,
and as we spilled out of our cars and gathered in the grassy
churchyard, Jim—who had established contact with our
hosts earlier—took time to introduce me.

The first person I met was a farmer whose bald head
glowed rose in the late afternoon sun, and whose face and
neck were burned beet-red from working in the fields. His
ill-fitting trousers were faded and worn. When he smiled,
two yellow canine teeth hung down to frame the black gap
where his missing front teeth used to be.

"Howdy, brother!" the farmer exclaimed in greeting. He
slapped me on the shoulder with his broad, calloused hand.
"Welcome to the Kingdom!"

I then turned to meet a woman who must have weighed
at least 300 pounds. She wore no makeup, and a telltale

bulge on her left jaw revealed a sizeable pinch of snuff carefully tucked between her gumline and lower lip. The woman greeted me jovially, and then—impulsively—embraced me.

"God loves you," she burbled. "And so do I!"

Instinctively, I pulled away. But before the woman would release me, she insisted on planting a big, wet, snuff-stained kiss on my cheek.

Reaching for my handkerchief to wipe away the brown stain, it occurred to me that if this odd assortment of characters was in any way representative of the citizenry of God's "Kingdom," I wasn't so sure I wanted to belong. Feeling ill at ease and out of place, I wondered what possible reason God could have had in calling me here.

At six o'clock the Mission formally commenced with a traditional covered-dish supper, Outer Banks style. Manteo church members had gone all out to prepare a stupendous array of down-home dishes: fresh-shucked oysters, barbequed shrimp, conch fritters, southern-fried chicken, all manner of home-grown, fresh-cooked vegetables, salads, slaw, steaming cornbread, and hot buttered biscuits. For dessert there was a seemingly endless assortment of homemade cakes, fresh fruit pies, cookies, and custards.

When everyone had eaten their fill and the tables had been cleared, we moved into the church sanctuary and Jim opened the first night of the Mission. To my surprise, he called on the farmer with the missing front teeth to offer the opening prayer.

Now hold on a minute! I thought. *This can't be right. Only ministers can pray.* Never before had I heard a lay person praying out loud in church—let alone a person seemingly so unqualified as this common man.

"Lord Jesus," the farmer began, "thank You for this opportunity You've given us all to be together. . . ."

As he continued, I was amazed to notice that he didn't pray "King James style," that is, using *thees* and *thous*, but he prayed in plain, simple conversational English. Never had I heard anyone pray in this manner before. It was as though the farmer were talking with someone he knew intimately—his brother, his father, his best friend.

The farmer closed by asking God to bless our efforts in this Lay Witness Mission, and to be with us in a real way. *Now that was a nice idea*, I thought. *But was there really a way that God could actually be with us?* Even after my experience at Basswood Lake, I'd continued to picture God as fixed in Heaven, regarding His creation from a great distance. *God with us? Here? In this room?* That was something new.

When the opening prayer had ended, song sheets were distributed, and under the direction of an ebullient song leader we commenced singing. These were new songs which I'd never heard before. Lighthearted and happy, they had a catchy beat. Some people even clapped as they sang. The lyrics were different, too. They told of Jesus and His power to save sinners. *Save sinners?* I'd always been under the impression that only Baptists got "saved."

Next, Jim called upon a woman who was seated toward the front of the room to "share with us what Jesus had done for her." It was my overweight friend who dipped snuff. *Now what could she possibly have to say?*

Explaining that she wasn't the best of speakers, the woman began by asking a friend who was sitting nearby to pray for her. The friend complied. Then haltingly, shyly, the woman began to tell us how two years earlier Jesus had come into her life and gradually transformed her from a depressed, self-pitying mess to the confident, happy person that she was today.

Never before had I heard the effect of Jesus on a person's life described in such a personal way. Like the farmer, it was as though the woman actually *knew* Jesus—as though He was her closest friend. Tears welled up in my eyes as I realized that God really did love this woman; because she had accepted His love, she had been empowered to love herself and others. Her words "God loves you, and so do I!" spoken when we first met, had not been mere religious jargon, but a heartfelt expression of what, for this woman, was the single most important truth she knew.

The remainder of the weekend—which included coffee group discussions, informal lectures, and additional chances for people to share their Christian testimonies— was thoroughly enjoyable and passed quickly.

Driving home, I found myself humming some of the new songs I had learned, and I was filled with a sense of joy and hope not unlike the way I had felt three years earlier, upon returning home from Basswood Lake.

God is alive! I felt as though my heart might burst with this good news. How wrong I had been in assuming that there was nothing I could learn from the people of Manteo. If anything, these good people seemed to have a far better grasp of what it meant to be a Christian than I had. I envied the ease and intimacy with which they talked to God in prayer. I yearned for the simple, yet deeply moving manner in which they shared their faith. I wished, also, that I was half as acquainted with the Bible as they were; many seemed to have the book nearly committed to memory.

And it wasn't only the folks in Manteo who had this special kind of relationship with God. As the weekend had progressed, I had noticed that Jim and several other members of our Lay Witness Mission team did, as well. *What was it about these people that made their religion so real?* I wondered. *After all, I believed in God. Didn't that make me a Christian, too?*

As I approached Durham's city limits, I had concluded that there was some crucial link missing in my understanding of Christianity. At times I felt so close to grasping the faith, and yet, at moments like this, so far away.

While unpacking my suitcase at home, I glanced through the several books that I had purchased during the weekend at the church's book table. One book in particular caught my eye—a thirty-five-cent paperback called *Good News for Modern Man*. The blurb on the cover described the book as "Today's English Version" of the New Testament. Figuring that any version of the Bible would be an improvement over my hard-to-understand King James, I was looking forward to reading it.

That night, it was with a pleasant sense of anticipation that I headed downstairs with my new copy of *Good News for Modern Man* and settled back in my favorite easy chair for an evening of reading. Even so, I was hardly prepared for what happened.

Beginning with the book of Matthew (the first of the four Gospels), and on through the Acts of the Apostles, Paul's letters to the various early and struggling churches, and John's apocalyptic Revelation—the Bible seemed to come alive!

When Jesus spoke, it was as though He were speaking directly to me. Likewise with Paul, John, and all the others. Every word of the book was rich with meaning. Captivated, I sat—oblivious to the passing time—and read the book through, from cover to cover. In coming weeks, I would read it again—two, three, and four more times.

Gradually, I came to understand that while it was God the Father who had revealed Himself to me at Basswood Lake, I had yet to become a bona fide Christian by acknowledging Jesus Christ as His only Son—a Son whose mission it had been to die for humankind's sins in order that all who believe in Him might be reconciled to God and given the gift of eternal life. I had yet, in a most fundamental way, to ask Jesus into my life as my personal Lord and Savior, thus receiving His indwelling Holy Spirit and being regenerated spiritually, or "born again." Obvious as these basic tenets of the Chrisitian faith were, I had never before fully understood them. I had never before fully grasped the centrality of the Person of Jesus to Christianity. Jesus, it would seem, was my missing link to God.

Most significant was the fact that now, with my new-found information and understanding, I was called to make the most important decision of my life.

Was Jesus who He claimed to be?

Was Jesus "God's only [begotten] Son" (John 3:18), "the way, the truth, and the life" (John 14:6)? To His questioning apostles He had stated, "No one goes to the Father except by me" (John 14:6) and "Anyone who is not for me is really against me" (Matthew 12:30). Finally, in the book of Acts it is written, "Salvation is to be found through him [Jesus] alone; in all the world there is no one else whom God has given who can save us" (Acts 4:12).

Such dogmatic statements as these caused me to stop and think. Certainly in today's pluralistic society, they would hardly be considered intellectually or socially acceptable. At the same time I had to remember that God is not concerned with a person's intellect or social standing, but with the redemption of his soul through saving faith in Christ.

Was Jesus who He claimed to be?

From all that I'd read and witnessed, I was convinced that He was.

6

Of Prodigals and Prayer

It was early March, 1970, and I was enroute by plane to Wauwatosa, Wisconsin, a Milwaukee suburb and the site for another Lay Witness Mission.

In the two years since visiting Manteo, I had become fully caught up in church life and had also begun noticing the marked difference between nominal or cultural Christians, and those who embraced a regenerate or personal faith.

Cultural Christians could be described as those persons who may be regular or semi-regular churchgoers but whose motivation for attending stem from guilt, tradition, or vague sentimental reasons. Cultural Christians are not inclined to discuss their religious beliefs because "religion is a private matter." They consider those who pursue such religious practices as reading the Bible, praying, and expressing enthusiasm about their faith at best as odd, and at worst as fanatical. Cultural Christians balk at such biblically derived spiritual concepts as man's inherent sinful nature, the on-going battle being waged between God and Satan for each person's soul, the uniqueness of Jesus, and the existence of Hell. Basically, they are people who feel that by being a good person, by working hard, and by cultivating a positive attitude toward life, one is assured a place in Heaven and eternal life with God—if there is a Heaven, if there is eternal life, if there is a God. Indeed, such had been the nature of my faith for most of my lifetime.

At any rate, it is, I think, because I perceived this difference between cultural and regenerate Christians that I grew so fond of participating in Lay Witness Missions. It was exciting and rewarding to share the gospel in a personal way, especially with those who had never before heard the good news. Even more thrilling was discovering— sometimes during the Mission weekend, sometimes not for months or years later—that as a result of our efforts, some person's life had been transformed, revitalized, made whole, through faith in Jesus.

In Wauwatosa, my hosts were Dr. Jack and Doris Olinger. Doris met me at the door.

"We are so happy that you will be staying with us for the weekend," she said warmly, showing me to her comfortable living room. "Jack should be home shortly. He's making his rounds at the hospital."

"Great!" I said. "I'm looking forward to meeting him. Being from the South, I'm curious to see how a doctor works 'way up here in Yankee land."

Doris smiled, though I noticed she seemed preoccupied.

Briefly, we told each other about our families, our homes, our work. After a while, I began to talk about the upcoming Lay Witness Mission at the Olingers' church, sharing my enthusiasm for the program and my hopes for the weekend. Doris responded politely. I sensed that she and her husband had become involved with the Mission more out of a sense of duty than anything else. In fact, from what I could gather, the Olingers appeared to be a classic example of cultural Christians—good, hard-working people, doing the best they could with what limited spiritual resources they had.

Soon I heard the sound of a back door slamming, and Jack appeared in the living room. He was a good-looking man—slim, wiry, alert.

"Nice to meet you." He extended his hand.

"Same here," I replied. "I was just telling Doris how much I was looking forward to meeting you."

Jack grinned. Then the slam of the back door announcing another arrival caused his expression to change abruptly.

It was Carl, the Olingers' teenage son. He would have filed past us without saying a word, had his mother not intercepted him.

"Carl," she said softly, "I want you to meet Dr. Wilson, from North Carolina. He's going to be one of the leaders at the Lay Witness Mission taking place at church this weekend."

"Hullo," mumbled Carl. He spoke in a monotone, refusing to let his eyes meet mine. His long hair was dirty and unkempt, as was his overall appearance. I'd counseled many young kids who were into drugs, and I wondered if this might be Carl's problem.

"Hi," I countered. "Think you'll be able to join us at the church this weekend? I hear there's going to be a great Youth Program taking place. Lots of kids have already signed up to attend."

"Maybe," replied Carl.

"*Maybe?*" echoed his father sharply. Jack's voice was cold, and his body visibly tensed as he waited for his son's reply.

"You heard me," said Carl evenly, deliberately avoiding his father's steely gaze. "Maybe."

With that, he turned and headed up the stairs.

In the moments following Carl's departure I feared the room might ignite should anyone speak, so loaded with tension was the atmosphere. Never had I witnessed such deep animosity and controlled hostility between a father and son; clearly the problem between Jack and Carl was too serious and deeply rooted to be explained away as the product of normal teenage rebellion. To complicate matters, I also sensed that while the conflict was primarily between father and son, poor Doris was trapped in the middle, locked in her thankless role as peacemaker. My heart went

out to this troubled family; though as a stranger, I knew
that for me to interfere would be inappropriate and unap-
preciated.

At 5:45 that evening, the Lay Witness Mission got off to
a good start with a traditional covered-dish supper. The
food was great, the singing joyful, and the testimonies
shared by selected team members seemed to me to be unusually moving. Occasionally I glanced in the direction of
the Olingers to notice how they were responding. They
seemed quite attentive, if not absorbed by the proceedings.
Even Carl, seated apart from his parents in the rear of the
room, seemed to be alert and interested.

Later that evening, joined by friends, we returned to the
Olingers' for coffee and cake. When the others had left,
Jack, Doris, and I talked for a while longer before retiring.
In the course of the evening we had gradually come to feel
more familiar with each other—more willing to open up and
share our personal lives. Still, the candor with which Jack
addressed me took me by surprise.

"I guess you've noticed the problem we've got with
Carl," he said quietly, as he slowly stirred his coffee.

Preferring to let him continue, I said nothing.

"It's hard to figure what went wrong," he said. "When
Carl was younger, we had no problems. No problems at all.
Then, when he was around thirteen, he started getting
rebellious. Ornery as hell. Then he got into drugs." He
paused, glancing at Doris, as if waiting for her go-ahead to
continue. She sat stiffly in her wing-backed chair, biting
her lower lip. For a moment I feared she might cry.

"Well, he got into drugs," Jack went on. "And it's been a
living nightmare for us ever since. He's unable to function
in a classroom environment, and we don't even know if he'll
be able to stay in school. He's left home several times, and
he refuses help of any kind." He shook his head. "God
knows I've tried to control him, but I can't. On more than
one occasion, we've come to physical blows. We just don't
know what to do."

For a moment Jack was silent. Then he continued.

"You know, Bill, I'm really surprised he's agreed to attend this Mission weekend at the church. I can't imagine why he's doing it."

"Maybe God wants him there," I said. "Maybe God wants to help him."

Jack regarded me quizzically, but said nothing.

The subject of Carl was abandoned.

The following day dawned cold and clear. In the morning, Jack, Doris, and I went our separate ways as we each attended coffee group meetings in the homes of several church members. The meetings were intended to provide a casual setting where the topic of prayer was discussed. At the same time, Carl was attending a day-long youth program.

Later on, Jack and I met again at the church for the men's luncheon, where the topic of discussion was how God plays a part in our work life.

After dessert, while coffee was being poured, I asked if anyone in the room might want to share, in an impromptu fashion, struggles or victories they had been experiencing through their Christian faith. After a momentary awkward silence, a visiting Catholic priest raised his hand. As this was primarily a Methodist Mission weekend, I wondered what had prompted this man to participate. I quickly found out.

Candidly, yet with great difficulty, the priest told us about feelings of guilt and conflict he was suffering over the prospect of giving up the priesthood because of his love for and upcoming marriage to a nun—a woman who was also suffering similar painful emotions. The priest was clearly troubled, so I asked if anyone in the room would like to pray for him. The men were surprisingly quick to respond with prayers that were both sensitive and sincere. From that moment on, it was as though a floodgate had been opened, and nearly a dozen others volunteered to share their stories. After some discussion and more prayers for those who expressed needs, the luncheon ended.

"Wow," remarked Jack, as we stood in the church foyer,

bundling up in overcoats and mufflers to face the cold out-
doors. "I've never experienced anything like that before. I
don't think I've ever heard men speak so openly. They
really seemed to trust and care for each other. And when
they prayed, it was as though they really believed that God
was listening."

"Isn't it great?" I responded. "I'm just beginning to learn
how healing it can be when a person prays with others
about his problems. From a psychiatrist's point of view, it's
fascinating."

"Yeah," replied Jack, though his voice sounded distant
and somewhat doubtful.

"Listen," I said, as we headed for the car. "We've got the
rest of the afternoon off, and I understand you've got some
rounds to make at the hospital. Mind if I join you?"

"You really don't have to," replied Jack. "I'll only be
gone a short while. Besides, wouldn't you rather use that
time to rest up?"

"Uh-uh," I said. "I enjoy visiting other hospitals. Patients, too. I promise I won't get in your way."

"Well," said Jack reluctantly, "if you really want to."

As we arrived at the hospital, Jack told me about one of
his most troublesome cases, a middle-aged woman with
cancer. In recent months the disease had spread like wild-
fire throughout her body, including several of her vital
organs. Just recently she had been told that she had only
six weeks to live. In response, she had become very depressed. In addition, the woman's daughter, who was in
her mid-thirties and unmarried, had also taken the news
very hard. In a classic response to her mother's impending
death, the daughter was angry, resentful, and frightened
at the prospect of being left alone in the world. Her father
had died some years earlier.

When we arrived at the sick woman's room, her daughter was visiting her. Tall, thin and plainly dressed, the
daughter's face was pinched and drawn. Her mother, too,
was the picture of despair. Gray and withered, she ap-

peared lost on the vast expanse of her white-sheeted bed. When Jack had concluded his examination of the woman, I talked to her for a while about her condition and her feelings. As Jack had indicated to me earlier, it was clear the woman was severely depressed. When our conversation had ended, the two of us sat in awkward silence. How desperately I wanted to offer her some message of hope and encouragement! But I could think of nothing to say.

Then, just as I was about to rise from my chair and prepare to leave, Jack spoke up.

"Dr. Wilson is a Christian physician," he said to the woman. "If you'd like, I know he would be happy to pray for you."

What?! I thought. *Pray for her? I've never prayed for a patient in my life, let alone considered such a thing.*

But it was too late to back out now. The woman was nodding yes, she'd like for me to pray for her. Swallowing hard, I tried not to appear flustered.

"Uh, thank You, Lord," I fumbled for words. "Thank You for letting us come to You in prayer. . . ."

Eventually, I concluded by asking God to comfort both the woman and her daughter, and to heal the woman as He saw fit. Whatever I said must not have been too inadequate, because as I stood to leave the woman reached out and took hold of my hand.

"Thank you, doctor," she said. "You've no idea what your prayer meant to me." Her eyes were moist with tears.

Two more times that afternoon Jack asked me to pray for patients; each time I complied, feeling that it was somehow the right thing to do. As we left the hospital and headed toward the car, I surmised that Jack assumed doctors who happened to be Christians prayed with their patients as a matter of course.

"So tell me," he said as we pulled out of the doctors' parking lot and began to drive home, "How is it that you came to be so religious? I mean, how can you be so sure of what you believe?"

I thought for a moment and then cited the scriptural references that indicated Jesus was humankind's missing link to God, stressing those passages that had been so meaningful to me in my search for truth.

This approach, however, brought up the issue of the authority of the Bible.

"How can you, a doctor, believe in a book so unscientific?" asked Jack. "Surely you're aware of the Genesis creation story, not to mention all those miracles. How can you reconcile such things with scientific knowledge?"

"Well," I replied slowly, "I guess I don't see reconciliation between the Bible and modern science as being the issue. If you ask me, both points of view, when taken to the extreme, lack ultimate veracity. If someone tells me the universe began with a Big Bang, what I want to know is, who set it off? If someone else tells me that God created the world in seven literal days, what I want to know is, how long is one day to God?"

"Fair enough," said Jack. "But I still don't understand how you can embrace a religion based on such an unscientific book."

"Jack," I replied, holding up my Bible with one hand, while pointing to it emphatically with the other, "you must remember that this book was written by men of faith, not men of science."

"Hm-m," said Jack thoughtfully.

We continued the remainder of our drive home in silence.

Later that evening, while attending the Saturday night session at the church, I had been wondering how Carl was getting along when I bumped into him—literally—in the second floor stairwell. With several other members of the youth group he had joined in the game of "Trust," a spiritual exercise wherein each player takes a turn at being blindfolded and led by another around the church—upstairs, downstairs, out-of-doors, and then back to the starting point. Through this exercise, Carl was hopefully not only learning how to trust others, but also how to trust in

God. Whatever Carl may have been learning from the game, I was glad to see that he seemed to be having a good time.

The next morning found me at the church bright and early, meeting with the other team members to prepare for the eleven o'clock Sunday morning worship service—the final scheduled event of our Lay Witness Mission in Wauwatosa. We wanted the service to be memorable for the congregation, so we decided to do things a little differently: At the end of the service, just prior to the invitation (this is the time when members of the congregation are invited to come forward to express or renew their commitment to Jesus) we would each take turns sharing a few words about what Jesus meant to us. I was slated to speak last.

As the service unfolded, I listened, misty-eyed, to the moving testimonies of my fellow team members. It had been a good weekend, I realized. A wonderful weekend. I was especially grateful for the opportunities I had had to try and communicate the gospel in an understandable way, and for the many new friends I'd made in the process—most notably the Olingers. Suddenly it was my turn to speak, and I found myself sharing a brief story about my days as an intern in the Panama Canal Zone.

"It was as an intern that I delivered my first baby," I recalled. "For those of you who've had an opportunity to witness a live birth, I guess you know that it's not exactly a pretty sight. The newborn is most always covered with blood and a waxy white coating that protects the baby during its strenuous passage through the birth canal. The child may also be bruised and its head misshapen from the process. To tell the truth, I was pretty shocked the first time I saw all this. But do you know what had an even greater effect on me? It was the mother's reaction.

"I say this because no matter how unsightly that newborn baby might have been to my eyes—no matter how bloody or bruised—the moment that child entered this world and was placed in his mother's arms, he was *loved*.

I'd never seen anything like it. In a most remarkable way,
the new mother's love for her child transcended all her
baby's imperfections."

For a moment I paused, considering the meaning of what
I was about to say.

"That's the way God's love is," I explained. "No matter
how dirty or ugly or bruised we may be, God loves us. With
all our failings, infirmities, and shortcomings, God loves us.
In a way no human being can, God loves us. All He asks of
us is that we somehow try to comprehend His great love for
us, and in response, love Him back."

As I returned to my seat, the invitation was given. "Just
As I Am," that grand old hymn, played softly on the organ
and a few people responded by leaving their seats and coming forward to kneel at the communion rail at the front of
the sanctuary. Some time passed, and a few more people
came forward. Then, a few more, until finally the communion rail was filled.

It was then that I noticed Carl, kneeling with his head
bowed, to the far left of the rail. To the far right, in the
same position, was Jack. In the middle, was Doris.

Suddenly, at precisely the same moment—as if carrying
out the work of a master choreographer—Jack and Carl
rose from their knees and turned to face each other. For a
moment Jack stared, visibly overcome by the emotion of
the moment, then rapidly crossed the room and embraced
his son. Carl, equally overcome, returned his father's embrace. For several moments the two of them stood locked
in each other's arms, father and son reconciled through the
love of God.

Tears filled my eyes, as I was struck by the scene's star-
tling resemblance to the parable of the Prodigal Son:

> "He was still a long way from home when his father saw him;
> his heart was filled with pity, and he ran, threw his arms
> around his son, and kissed him. 'Father,' the son said, 'I have
> sinned against God and against you. I am no longer fit to be
> called your son.' But the father called to his servants. 'Hurry!'
> he said. 'Bring the best robe and put it on him. Put a ring on

his finger and shoes on his feet. Then go and get the prize calf and kill it, and let us celebrate with a feast! For this son of mine was dead, but now he is alive; he was lost, but now he has been found'" (Luke 15:20–24).

While I knew that God was in the business of healing broken relationships, I was still amazed that He could bridge a chasm so deep as that which had separated Jack and Carl. God, it seemed, had accomplished in one weekend what months and years of psychiatric counseling and therapy might never have achieved. Thanks to the Olingers, I had truly learned in an unforgettable way the Lord's power to transform and reorient believers' lives. (Carl, I should mention, completely got off drugs and continued with his education to become an electrical engineer. So profound was the effect of Christianity in the lives of Jack and Doris that they eventually moved from Wauwatosa to the Amazonian basin of Ecuador as medical missionaries.)

I also made another valuable observation during my weekend in Wauwatosa. When I made rounds with Jack in the hospital I saw the great healing power of prayer. (Later I would learn that though the woman with cancer did die from her malignancy, she was able to leave this world without sadness or fear, and with a meaningful faith. Her daughter, as a result, became a believer, and went on to live a productive and happy life as a single person. My prayers for the other two patients were answered in an equally positive manner.)

Mulling these things over on the flight home to Durham, I grew increasingly convinced that inconvenient as it may be, the time had come for me to attempt to integrate my faith—which I knew from first-hand experience to be valid—with my profession.

"Thank You, Lord," I murmured, as the plane touched down in Durham, "for all You taught me this weekend. Help me now to somehow begin to apply what I've learned to my practice. Teach me what it means to be a Christian physician."

7

To Touch the Hem of His Garment

It was a drizzly summer afternoon, and I was sitting in my office at the hospital awaiting the arrival of my next patient. Though only a few weeks had passed since my visit with the Olingers in Wauwatosa, it seemed more like a century. Wistfully, I recalled my original enthusiasm and resolve to put to practice all that I had learned that extraordinary weekend.

While I remained convinced of the helpfulness that conversion and prayer played in healing, I was stymied as to how to begin to integrate these principles in my work. Patients came and patients went, and still I was no closer to understanding what it meant to be a Christian psychiatrist.

Certain aspects of my personal life, too, were in a rut. My temper, especially, continued to be an annoying problem. No matter how hard I tried to remain cool in stressful situations, it seemed that inevitably and in the most inopportune moments, I'd lose control. While such episodes were disturbing enough when they involved my students and associates, the ones that bothered me the most were those that took place at home. Elizabeth, as was her nature, was tolerant and patient. But recently the two of us had decided to try praying about my bad temper with the hope that with God's help I might be healed.

My thoughts were interrupted by the buzz of the intercom on my desk.

"Naomi's here," announced the receptionist. "Are you ready to see her?"

Naomi! The mere mention of the woman's name caused me to tense with frustration and weariness. Talk about a hopeless case of anger!

Naomi was a middle-aged woman who had been visiting me every two weeks for more than a year. Her problem was uncontrollable anger—the likes of which I'd never known—manifested by hostile behavior toward men, both at home and on the job.

It is likely that Naomi's problem stemmed from the time when she was twelve years old and subjected to repeated episodes of sexual abuse from her brother-in-law. Upon confronting her parents about the problem, Naomi received no sympathy or help; instead, she was wrongly accused of "leading the brother-in-law on," and therefore being to blame. It was then that the seeds of her bitterness were sown.

Years later, Naomi married. Though she had two children and was married to a man who loved her very much, she grew increasingly frustrated in coping with her husband's progressive and incurable case of impotence. Naomi's frustration turned into anger—albeit carefully repressed—which ultimately was vented by outbursts of rage toward many men associated with her husband's business. Some years later Naomi went to work herself, only to find that she was inexplicably hostile toward her male coworkers.

Because of her uncontrollable outbursts, Naomi was referred by her doctor to a psychiatrist. After several sessions it was recommended that she undergo psychosurgery—a drastic treatment involving the cutting of fiber tracks in the brain, and generally regarded as a measure to be considered only as a last resort. Quite understandably, Naomi refused. For the next twenty years she lived in misery, incapacitated by her anger and by the frightful notion that she was insane.

It wasn't long after Naomi came into my care that I

realized I would unlikely be able to help her. While I listened to her problems and did my best to offer comfort, her anger was such that I didn't know how to handle it.

Now she entered my office—a deceptively sweet-looking woman with a soft laugh and the rosy-cheeked face of an angel. In all truth, Naomi was a lovely person—until the surface of her anger was scratched.

Today Naomi was angry at her fellow workers, and we spent the first thirty minutes of our hour together reviewing all that had transpired at her job since I'd last seen her. As I listened to Naomi recount the innumerable wrongs that she felt had been committed against her, I found myself wondering, as I always did during our sessions, what the missing key could be to curing her anger. *How*, I asked myself, *does one go about defusing such a deep-seated and destructive emotion?*

As I meditated on this question, it suddenly occurred to me that the only way Naomi could be healed of her anger would be to somehow find it in her heart to *forgive* all the persons, real or imagined, who she believed had hurt her over the years. At the same time, I knew that most people—especially a person as angry as Naomi—are incapable of forgiving on their own strength; the *power* to forgive comes exclusively from God. There was my answer! In order to be empowered to forgive, and thus be healed of her anger, Naomi needed God.

It all sounded so simple. Yet within the confines of my office—its walls decorated with diplomas, awards, and various meritorious certificates of my profession—such an approach seemed wildly improbable. Still, it was better than anything I'd been able to come up with in the past. In truth, it was all I had to offer.

"Naomi," I interrupted softly.

She regarded me curiously.

"Tell me something." I drew a deep breath. "Are you a Christian?"

"Of course!" she snapped indignantly. "I go to church every Sunday!"

"But do you have a personal relationship with Jesus?" I asked. "Does your faith in Him help you in any real way?"

For a moment Naomi was silent. Then, in a low voice, she replied, "I guess not."

"The reason I'm asking you these questions," I explained, "is to find out if you have the power within you to free yourself from your anger. The only way I can ever help you is to bring you to the point where you are capable of forgiving all the people with whom you are angry, not only those you've mentioned today, but all those from the past, too. Do you realize how your resentment and bitterness toward those individuals keep you captive in your own misery?" I asked.

Naomi nodded numbly, tears filling her eyes.

I went on to explain how the only way she could obtain the power to forgive was to accept Jesus and allow His Holy Spirit to enter her life.

"I asked you a moment ago if you felt you had a personal relationship with Jesus. You indicated you didn't." I paused, not quite believing what I was about to ask her. "Would you like to?"

Naomi was very quiet. Then, the hope of all the world carried in her tremulous voice, she responded.

"Oh yes, Dr. Wilson," she cried. "Yes, I would!"

As luck would have it, I happened to have in my desk drawer a copy of *Four Spiritual Laws*, the booklet developed by the Campus Crusade for Christ organization, which instructs the reader how to become a Christian through four basic steps documented by Scripture.

Together Naomi and I went through the booklet, step-by-step, until we arrived at the closing prayer. After reading the prayer silently, Naomi decided she wanted to say it with me out loud:

"Lord Jesus," she read. "I need You. Thank You for dying on the cross for my sins. I open the door of my life and receive You as my Savior and Lord. Thank You for forgiving my sins and giving me eternal life. Take control

of my life. Make me the kind of person You want me to be."*

"What I want to know," she smiled when she had finished, tucking the booklet in her handbag, "is why no one ever told me about Jesus before!"

From that day on, Naomi began to change dramatically. Forgiveness, indeed, proved to be the key to curing her anger; and, for many sessions after her conversion, we probed her past, seeking to recall all those who had hurt her, intentionally or unintentionally, and then forgiving them one by one. It was a painstaking process, but Naomi was eventually healed. In time, no longer did anger and rage plague her emotional life. No longer did she have problems relating to men at work. Best of all, a loving relationship between Naomi and her husband was reestablished, and their marriage was saved.

Naomi's case represented a landmark achievement in my quest to integrate my faith with my work. Not only did it further substantiate my growing conviction that regeneration of the spirit through conversion was not only helpful but necessary for healing, it also revealed the remarkable effectiveness of *prayer* as a valuable therapeutic tool. From that time on, I always made certain to pray with and for all my patients—if not out loud in their presence, then silently.

Another reason Naomi's case impressed me was because it bore such similarities to my own problem. If Naomi could be healed of her anger—far more deep-seated and destructive than my own—why couldn't I?

Several weeks after Naomi's conversion, I found my answer.

Joined by Elizabeth and six kids—three of our own, and three belonging to friends—I was piloting our eight-passenger van on rain-slicked Interstate 40, en route from Durham to a Lay Witness Mission weekend in Red Bank,

---

Tennessee, just outside Chattanooga. Nearing the North
Carolina town of Asheville, I pulled into a service station.

"Fill 'er up," I said to the attendant. "And I'd appreciate
it if you could clean the windshield, too."

At first I thought the attendant hadn't heard me, so
vacant was his countenance. But after placing the gas hose
in our tank, he returned to the front of the van carrying an
old rag and grimy plastic bottle of cleaning fluid. As I observed him half-heartedly drag the rag across the windshield, leaving long murky streaks, I felt myself growing
annoyed. I've never had patience with mediocrity. I'm the
type of person who expects people to do a good job—be it a
lab technician taking an electroencephalograph reading or a
gas station attendant cleaning a windshield.

"Hey," I rolled down my window and gestured with my
hand toward the still-dirty windshield. "As long as you're
at it, why not try to do a good job?"

While my tone was admittedly sarcastic, I hardly expected the attendant's response.

"You want the job done good?" he snarled. "Then do it
yourself!" He threw the dirty rag into a nearby trash can,
and disappeared to the back of the van.

Though I felt my face growing hot with anger, I was
determined to stay calm. I would not allow this sullen attendant to get under my skin. I would not embarrass my
wife and the kids with a scene.

Summoning all my self-control, I paid the attendant
without a word, pulled the van out onto the Interstate, and
tried to forget the incident.

Upon arriving in Red Bank, we pulled into another service station—only to discover that our gas cap was missing.
The attendant in Asheville had either failed to tighten it or
maliciously decided not to replace it after filling our tank.
Assuming the latter, I was furious—so furious that the
incident almost ruined my weekend. While we were able to
purchase another gas cap, it didn't fit properly, and every
time I looked at it my fury toward the attendant mounted.

By the end of the weekend, I had determined that on the way home I would make a special stop in Asheville to reclaim my gas cap, which I was certain the attendant had.

As we pulled into the station and I caught sight of the unsuspecting attendant, my heart started pounding. To my surprise, he didn't seem to recognize me.

"What'll it be?" he asked.

"What'll it be?" I snapped. "I don't suppose you know anything about our missing gas cap?"

"Huh?" The man responded dully, as though he didn't know what I was talking about.

"Our gas cap," I growled. "The one you forgot to screw on properly when we stopped here two days ago. The one we lost and had to replace."

"Sorry, mister. I don't know what you're talking about." He frowned. "You better calm down, or you're likely to have a heart attack."

That did it.

"*Calm down?!*" I yelped. "*Calm down?*" I opened my door and stepped out of the van. "Where's the manager? I want to speak to the manager."

"Sorry, mister," said the attendant. "He's not here."

"Not here?" I screeched. "Then where's the owner? I want to speak to the owner."

"Sorry, mister. He's not here either."

"Then give me the owner's phone number."

"Sorry, mister, I don't even know the owner's name."

By now, Elizabeth had gotten out of the van and was standing beside me.

"Bill," she said, pulling at my shirtsleeve. "Please let's go. Please don't get all upset. It's not worth it."

Furious, I pulled my arm away.

Noticing a name above the station's door, I assumed it to be the owner's. Determined to call him, I marched to a nearby phone booth, found his home phone number in the local directory, and placed the call. He was no help, either.

As I hung up the phone, still consumed with anger, I was

suddenly silenced by that still, small voice which I had come to know as God.

"Look at you," He said—not accusingly, but with immeasurable disappointment. "Just look at you."

I know Lord, I replied. *I've really gone and done it this time, haven't I?*

He said nothing.

Humiliated, I stepped back into the van and started the engine. Exhausted and shaken, I drove away.

As we headed east on Interstate 40, the only sound that could be heard was that of the engine and the rush of the tires on the road. No one spoke, so fearful were they of how I might react. As we drove along in tension-filled silence, I grew more and more uncomfortable. Like a swimmer caught in an undertow, I felt myself drowning in the overwhelming weight of shame and remorse that I felt for my behavior. It was the same old story. Once again my temper had gotten the better of me. When would it ever end?

I'm sorry, Lord, I prayed silently. *I really am.*

No sooner had the words passed through my mind, when it occurred to me that to apologize to God for my temper was something I had never done. In the past, I may have expressed my sorrow to persons I had offended—but never before to God.

For the next three hours—all the way from Asheville to Greensborough—I prayed about this when suddenly, just as I was turning onto Interstate 85 for the home stretch to Durham, I experienced a tremendous sense of relief, of renewal, of being made clean. At the same time I felt a tremendous surge of hope, of new resolve for the future. *I had been forgiven.*

Like Naomi, through the power of God's forgiveness, I was in the early stages of being set free from the bondage of my bad temper. While I knew that it would be premature to say that I would never lose my temper again, I did feel certain that from now on my outbursts would take place less frequently and with less intensity—and in time, perhaps not at all.

For the remainder of the drive home, I continued to pray, thanking God for the healing He'd worked in me so far, and for the ways He was teaching me to apply all that I was learning about Him to others through my profession. Though I sensed that what I had grasped so far about the healing power of God's love was merely the hem of His garment—so to speak—that was all right by me. At least it was a start.

8

To Be a Christian Physician

It was spring, 1972. Seven years had passed since my conversion experience at Basswood Lake. For many months now I had continued my search for a comprehensive approach to integrating Christianity with psychiatry, but with unremarkable results. While I knew that my theory that Christianity was beneficial—not detrimental—to mental health, was valid, I was reluctant about discussing it with my peers due to my lack of empirical evidence. More to the point, I was afraid of being summarily dismissed as a kook.

Never had my cowardice in this regard more acutely been brought home than one bitter cold Saturday afternoon in Chicago, a few weeks earlier. . . .

It was mid-winter, 1972, and I was serving as supervisor for the Board of Examiners engaged in testing candidates for certification in neurology and psychology at the Illinois Psychiatric Institute. As was typical during such events, participating physicians often shared meals together and engaged in professional shop talk.

On that particular Saturday, while eating lunch with several of the country's leading psychiatrists, we somehow got on the subject of religion. To my dismay, it was the general concensus of this distinguished group that "faith in God or Jesus is delusional; a person is crazy if he or she believes."

No! I wanted to leap from my seat and cry out. *That's*

not true! There is a God! He is real! He does heal! But, censored by my own fear, I said nothing. Finally, unable to stand it any longer, I excused myself from the table and left the restaurant to take a long walk.

Lord, I prayed, blinking back tears from both my distressed state and the bitter winter wind, *Help me not to be ashamed or afraid to share with others what I know to be true about Your reality and Your ways. Help me to be obedient to You in this regard—not from a sense of fear or begrudging duty, but from my love for You. Lord, I so want to be obedient. But You've got to help me. You've got to show me what it is You want me to do.* As I ended my prayer, once again my spirit was aware of the still small voice of God.

"What is it that you do best?" He asked.

Teach and do research, I replied.

"Then go and do those things to My glory!" He said.

Now, with that command ringing in my mind, I found myself back at square one: Somehow I had to find a way to communicate to my peers, patients, and students that Christianity was beneficial to mental health. No longer did the prospect of doing this intimidate me. No longer did I care what other people thought. As my defensiveness dissolved like the morning mist, I rolled up my sleeves and got to work.

For starters, I knew I had to thoroughly research all that had been documented about God's intervening healing power—from anecdotal information to the few items existing in the medical literature. With renewed interest, I reviewed my own tentative efforts in this largely unexplored field—most notably the research I had completed over the past year with Jim Timmons, a fourth-year medical student. Jim, a Christian, was also interested in integrating his faith with his career and had asked if he might work with me as a clinical elective. Together we had inquired into the religious lives of thirty patients. Ten suffered depression, ten had inoperable cancer, and ten were alcoholics. After inquiring into the patients' religious histories and spending considerable time in interviews, we made several interesting observations.

We began our study with the alcoholics. As we interviewed the first man, an overweight, red-faced construction worker, it was apparent that he suffered many deep inner hurts. The man described for us in detail the extent of his drinking and how it had contributed to his abusing his children and his wife, committing adultery, and gambling away his earnings. He described his religious life as nonexistent. When the interview had been completed, I went back and summarized for him the disastrous toll that alcoholism had taken on his life. To my dismay, the man began to cry. Upon regaining his composure, he admitted that he was in despair. Though he knew that the things he had done were morally wrong, he felt that he was helpless to control his behavior. For the remaining nine alcoholics, the story was much the same.

Jim examined the cancer patients on his own. He returned from the interviews to tell me that several of the patients were regenerate Christians, and that their attitude toward their life-threatening disease was quite different from those people who were nominal or cultural Christians, or who had no faith at all. The believers seemed to be able to cope better psychologically. They did not seem to be in as much despair about death because of their strongly held belief in an afterlife.

Finally, Jim and I interviewed the depressed patients. Many of them suffered biologically determined depressions; this kind of depression is also known as a major affective disorder or the depression half of manic-depressive illness. It is caused by a probable biochemical/physiological dysfunction in the brain. A few suffered neurotic depressions; this kind of depression, a learned overresponse to stimuli in life, is usually caused by parents who unintentionally or deliberately teach their offspring to respond in such a manner. Three of the patients, however, suffered a different kind of depression. These patients were severely depressed because their lives had no meaning, and they felt trapped in their sense of purposelessness. While I recognized mild existential depression as a common malady of successful people, I had not known it could be so severe as to bring individuals to want to commit suicide.

In my ongoing search for information, the books of Paul Tournier, the eminent Swiss psychiatrist and Christian, were very helpful, but they did not answer all my questions. The work of Quentin Hyder, a New York City–based psychiatrist, and also a Christian, added more understanding, but I still was not satisfied. A year passed, until one spring day in 1973, I received a letter that read something like this:

Dear Dr. Wilson:

I am a junior medical student at Temple University in Philadelphia. I want to be a Christian psychiatrist. I understand that you are a Christian psychiatrist. May I come and work with you?

Yours in Christ,
Dave Larson

Immediately, I wrote Dave back and invited him to spend the summer working with me, but he was already obligated to a job in Philadelphia. Further negotiations led to his agreeing to come to do an elective with me the next spring. Because of the financial strain that such a move imposed on Dave, I impulsively suggested that he come and live with our family during his twelve-week stay at Duke. He agreed, and I eagerly waited for his arrival.

From the moment Dave arrived, our children adopted him like a brother. A tall, muscular, clear-eyed Scandinavian, his energy was boundless. Outgoing and enthusiastic, he helped the children with their studies, he played with the little ones, he teased our daughters—all the while sharing his deep faith in a most loving and natural way. These traits, plus Dave's comprehensive knowledge of the Bible, enriched all our lives immeasurably.

In his work, as well, Dave was outstanding. He read more than what was asked of him. He interviewed patients in depth and then returned to ask me remarkably discerning questions—questions which further challenged me to determine how I could better integrate Christianity with psychiatry. Conveniently, I was at this time being referred to an increasing number of Christian patients with psychiatric problems. Dave's penetrating questions about these individuals resulted in long discussions and, ultimately, in our formulations and re-formulations of theories for a uniquely Christian system of psychotherapy.

As Dave and I talked, we became increasingly aware of the need for a starting point. From the outset, I recognized that Christian psychotherapy could only exist within the given understanding that there is, in fact, an omnipresent and omniscient God who has revealed Himself to humankind through His Son, Jesus Christ, and through His Word, the Bible, and who can also further reveal Himself to a person through the indwelling of His Holy Spirit. Such a presupposition implies, of course, that for the person who cannot believe or accept this given, Christian psychotherapy might seem at best delusional, and at worst a hoax. But such was to be expected; in Paul's letter to the Corinthians, he wrote, "For the message about Christ's death on the cross is nonsense to those who are being lost; but for us who are being saved it is God's power" (1 Cor. 1:18). I myself had no choice but to adhere to the reality of the healing power of God's love. I'd witnessed its effectiveness too many times, both in my own life and in the lives of others, to conclude otherwise.

It was also clear that if I hoped to identify a truly Christian system of psychotherapy, I could not begin by taking various Christian dynamics (such as conversion, repentance, confession, forgiveness, and so on) and attempting to "validate" them according to their correlation with existing psychiatric knowledge. Such an approach would be nothing less than absurd in that all scientific knowledge is in a constant state of flux—ever-changing and evolving with the passage of time. Quite the contrary, assuming that *God* is the fixed source of all perfect, permanent knowledge, what I had to do was: 1) determine God's view of the nature of man (as opposed to man's view of the nature of man—of which there exist as many views as there are those who choose to develop them); and 2) using the Bible as a base, construct a biblical framework against which I could correlate and validate existing secular truths from medicine, psychiatry, psychology, sociology, anthropology, and other related sciences.

Defining the nature of man from God's point of view as revealed in the Bible was not an easy task. Dave and I spent long days and nights searching the Scriptures on this subject and then comparing our findings with current medical and psychiatric knowledge. After much research, we determined that the nature of man in God's eyes consists of three dimensions: *body*, *soul*, and *spirit*. In Paul's letter to the Thessalonians he writes, "May the God who gives us peace make you holy in every way and keep your whole being—spirit, soul, and body—free from every fault . . ." (1 Thess. 5:23). This three-dimensional concept of man was very interesting, as the classic scientific definition of man is as a two-dimensional or bio-psychological being. Consideration of man's *spirit* is traditionally totally disregarded.

As a physician, I was well-acquainted with man's *body*. The body is more than the house in which we live. It is also made up of the biological drives such as sex, sleep, and appetite. These drives were referred to by the apostle Paul as *sarx*, or "the flesh." While it is true that these involuntary drives can be more or less inhibited, they are completely controlled only with great difficulty. The body is, of course, subject to disease, aging, and ultimately death.

Upon researching man's *soul*, Dave and I first encountered difficulties. I already knew that in standard textbooks of psychiatry and psychology, the word *soul* is not used, and even in theological circles the concept of soul has suffered a partial eclipse. Psychiatrists and psychologists prefer to use the word *psyche*, or the Freudian psychological terms *ego* and *super-ego*, or the even more vague concept of *self*. Sir John Eccles, the famous Australian neurophysiologist, preferred to term *psyche*. Historically, the most outstanding modern psychological thinker to consider the soul was Carl Jung. Yet in his considerations he never specifically defined what he meant when using the term. One gains the impression, however, that Jung considered the terms *soul*, and *psyche* to be synonomous.

Was there, then, validity in this seeming abandonment of the concept of soul? Or could the soul, in fact, be defined? After much investigation, I concluded that the soul could be defined. At the turn of the century, the Reverend Henry Lincicome listed a number of faculties found in man's soul, which readily translate to modern psychological concepts. The most important of these are: 1) emotions; 2) intellect, including memories and the emotions they elicit; 3) values we have learned; and 4) cognitive or reasoning abilities. Any psychiatrist would agree that it is these characteristics that make up a person's "psyche," or "self," or— as I prefer to call it—*soul*. Like the body, the soul is subject to disease. This kind of disease we commonly refer to as mental illness which is psychological, as opposed to biological, in origin.

So far, so good. But what about man's *spirit?* Only rarely in the scientific literature could Dave and I find anything even remotely alluding to this third dimension of man. Still, it was essential for our purposes that we try to define the spirit and determine whether it too, like the body and the soul, was subject to disease.

Some years ago, psychologist Joseph Jastrow observed that within all animal life there is an animating drive called the *élan vitale*, or life force. It is this force that imparts life to all living organisms, especially animals. It is the force that activates the cilia of the paramecium or creates eddies and flow in protoplasm. It is the force that prompts the migration of birds and drives man to explore his solar system. In addition, this life force provides a *tonus*—an internally generated emotional state that can be neutral, pleasant, or unpleasant. This life force, or *spirit*—as I prefer to call it—affects every function of the mind. In this sense, it is even more fundamental in its influence on man's thoughts and behavior than are man's biological drives.

Perhaps our most exciting discovery was that the spirit—like the body and the soul—is also subject to disease. Dave and I began to learn that there are diseases that arise within the spirit, and there are those that affect the spirit secondarily. Because there was nothing in the literature at that time that focused on spiritual pathology, we could only hypothesize in this regard. Later, however, I learned that diseases that arise within the spirit include alcoholism and existential depression. Existential depression (or despair) can occur in three different forms: 1) despair of meaning (a sense of purposelessness in life); 2) despair of morality (the despair that comes from failing to adhere to a value system, or from lacking a value system altogether); and 3) despair of death. In a sort of vicious pathological circle, it is these same diseases that affect the spirit secondarily. It should be noted that it is through conversion, wherein a person receives a new and Holy Spirit, that one most often is truly healed of these diseases.

Even though Dave and I had now determined a biblical, three-dimensional view of man, three more terms remained to be defined: *mind, will,* and *heart.*

An exhaustive search of the Bible and the secular scientific literature revealed that the most consistent definition of *mind* is that it is the noncorporeal or supernatural part of man, including man's biological drives, soul (or psyche), and spirit—plus the empowering quality of man's *will.* The *will,* as best can be determined, is the compound function of man's spirit and soul. The biblical term *heart* is a collective term for all of man's various emotions.

Having determined God's three-dimensional view of man, and having satisfactorily dealt with related terminology, I was eventually able to determine a uniquely Christian system of psychotherapy through which exciting and remarkable results were obtained with many of my patients. (See Parts II and III of this book.) Finally, employing sophisticated research techniques, I was also able to begin collecting data that served to document that Christianity is in fact not detrimental, but beneficial to mental health.

News of my research and of my success with heretofore hopeless cases spread rapidly. In time, associates were dropping by my office to chat about my method of therapy. Medical schools and professional organizations began asking me to speak on the subject of Christian psychiatry. By far the most exciting development was the demand by many of my students to teach them all I had learned. As a result, I began offering an elective course called "Christianity, Medicine, and Psychiatry," which proved to be extremely popular. This, however, turned out to be just the first step toward my ultimate goal.

In 1976, we established at Duke University a Program of Christianity in Medicine, which offers students comprehensive study, opportunities for supervised research, and counseling experience in this exciting field. The demand is such that nearly one-hundred students from nearly twenty different medical schools will have completed the course by the end of the 1983–84 school year.

To quote from the Program's brochure:

Christianity is a unique religious system in that it makes all mankind the object of everyman's concern. Its major focus is on the well-being, the wholeness, of each man. . . .

In today's world, where modern technology has made so

many mechanical advances, medical education and practice have lost sight of their [spiritual] origins. Concern for professionalism has often replaced concern for the human being; attention to technique and procedure has superceded attention to the whole person and his feelings; and somewhere along the way, love has been dropped from the medical vocabulary.

There is a need, then, to re-introduce and emphasize the positive aspects of Christian love and caring in medicine. Young Christian medical workers need to be encouraged in the practice of Christian medicine—to serve as much-needed leaven for all facets of the medical world.

It should be understood that I do not consider myself a sole innovator in the field of Christian psychiatry; other dedicated and farseeing people were pioneers long before I was. But it is exciting to share with them, and with you, this wonderful discovery and conviction that religion and psychiatry really can work together to mend broken lives.

PART II

WHEN SALVATION IS NOT ENOUGH

The Key to Wholeness:
Christian Psychotherapy

The Key to Wholeness: Christian Psychotherapy

The title of this section implies that there is such a thing as Christian psychotherapy, and that it differs significantly from secular forms of therapy. A casual reader of the literature on Christian psychology or pastoral counseling might not be convinced that there is a distinctively Christian form of psychotherapy, because many Christian therapists use primarily secular methods. Only a few writers of this literature begin with the Bible as a distinctive base and describe a counseling technique based on biblical teachings. It is from their articles and books, and from my own work, that I have attempted to determine what constitutes specifically Christian psychotherapy.

CURRENT TRENDS IN PSYCHOTHERAPY: A BRIEF REVIEW

Today's psychiatrists have many sophisticated tools with which to work in treating mental illness—drug therapy and electric-shock therapy, to name two. It is psychotherapy, however, that is best known by the lay public and that certainly gets the most attention. Indeed for many, to be in therapy is to be in vogue. Most everyone has at some time relished playing novice therapist to friends and family. Thanks largely to the pop media—in particular to the recent popularity of self-help books—"psychobabble" prevails.

In scientific circles, too, the categories and controversies of various psychotherapies are mind-boggling. In a recent overview of currently used methods, T. B. Karasu, psychoanalyst at the Albert Einstein School of Medicine in New York City, noted that at least 140 claim to be distinctive. After discussing the differences claimed for each, Karasu was able to reduce the 140 varieties of psychotherapies into three basic groups: 1) dynamic, 2) behavioral, and 3) experiential.

In order to fully understand the nature of Christian psychotherapy, it is important to have a fundamental knowledge of Karasu's three basic groups, briefly described as follows:

The *dynamicists* embrace concepts Freudian in origin. Their major emphasis is sexual repression. They maintain that all mental illness is caused by early unconscious sexual drives and wishes that are in conflict. They maintain that resolution of these underlying conflicts will result in mental health.

The *behavioralists'* major emphasis is anxiety. They maintain that all human behavior, healthy and unhealthy, is learned; mental illness is the result of excess or deficient behavior that has been environmentally reinforced. For the behavioralists, a person experiences mental health when there is absence of symptoms or reduced anxiety.

The *experientialists'* major emphasis is alienation. They define mental illness in terms of existential despair, fragmentation of self, and lack of acceptance of one's life experiences. They define mental health in terms of "self-actualization," which is the catalyst for personal growth.

Because the proponents of differing psychotherapies each tend to overemphasize certain aspects of their methods, it is difficult to determine where their claims have merit, and whether significant differences really do exist. Recognizing this, Karasu has taken the helpful approach of ascribing to each system of analysis several specific components, thus producing some order out of the chaos. This approach also provides a standardized framework within which different psychotherapies can be objectively compared and evaluated. It is this framework I have used in formulating the following overview of Christian psychotherapy.

MAN IN GOD'S EYES

As I have mentioned earlier in this book, the starting point or foundation of all psychotherapies is a concept of the nature of man. To recap, the Bible teaches that man consists of three dimensions: *body*, *soul*, and *spirit*.

> May the God who gives us peace make you holy in every way and keep your whole being—spirit, soul, and body—free from every fault . . . (1 Thess. 5:23).

Unfortunately, it would seem that most modern therapists have a rather limited understanding of man's nature and of the factors determining human behavior. The best secular effort made to date to formulate a concept of man's nature has been that of Sigmund Freud, who divided it into three parts: 1) the *id* (primarily sexual drives), 2) the *ego* (that part of the psyche which experiences the external world and which consciously controls the impulses of the id), and 3) the *super-ego* (that part of the psyche which controls at an unconscious level the impulses of the id). Freud's concept ignores completely the spiritual dimension of man's nature, and includes only incomplete ideas of the body and the soul.

The behavioralists offer an even narrower concept of man, for they recognize only the soul. As they believe all behavior is learned, what they do with the biological drives of the body, and with the spirit, is not clear; at best it can be said that they acknowledge their existence, but deny their significance.

The experientialists, on the other hand, focus on the experiential moment—on man's "being" in the here and now. This could be considered a primarily "spiritual" emphasis, but it also tends to nearly totally exclude consideration of the body and the soul.

Paul Tournier, who is considered by many to be the dean of Christian psychotherapists, has based his counseling approach on a holistic view of man. He has chosen to view man biblically, and has also postulated that man's nature consists of three dimensions: *body, psyche,* and *mind.* According to Tournier, the *body* includes the instincts, appetites, and physiological functions. It grows old, gets sick, and dies. The *psyche* is the dimension of man that experiences emotion and is able to imagine things. The *mind* is the dimension that thinks, reasons, wills, and deals with abstract ideas.

Tournier's ideas differ in many details from those of other Christian writers, but the major problem as I see it, is the fact that his view of man fails to include the all-important dimension of man's *spirit;* although, he is aware of the transcendental and does emphasize its role. Nevertheless, Tournier's theories and techniques have had a profound influence on the field of Christian psychotherapy largely, I believe, because he reconciles secular and biblical concepts in a way that serves to reveal the essential truths of both.

Man, however, *does have a spirit.*

It is at this level that God communicates with man, and man with God. As mentioned earlier, only the experientialists take into account the possible existence of a prime mover, which they perceive as some vague universal consciousness. In contrast, Christian psychotherapy is based on the certain knowledge that a prime mover does indeed exist and that He is more than a vague consciousness. He is God, the One who two-thousand years ago manifested Himself on earth in the form of His Son, Jesus Christ. This

Jesus died, was resurrected, and, after returning to the Father, sent His Holy Spirit to His believers to reveal truth, give power, and fill them with an active love for their fellow humans.

God is experienced transcendentally by man in two ways. First, through His Holy Spirit.

> We have not received this world's spirit; instead, we have received the Spirit sent by God, so that we may know all that God has given us . . . .
> Whoever does not have the Spirit cannot receive the gifts that come from God's Spirit. Such a person really does not understand them; they are nonsense to him, because their value can be judged only on a spiritual basis (1 Cor. 2:12, 14).

Second, God is experienced transcendentally through His Word, the Bible.

> All Scripture is inspired by God and is useful for teaching the truth, rebuking error, correcting faults, and giving instruction for right living, so that the person who serves God may be fully qualified and equipped to do every kind of good deed (2 Tim. 3:16–17).

In the Bible, God has provided guidelines for right living and emotional discipline, and He has given man a set of values that will make a favorable difference in his life. One of the most important concepts in the Christian belief system, however, is that God gives His followers the *power* to live out these values, through the presence of His indwelling Holy Spirit. This gift of the Holy Spirit was promised to all believers by Jesus, when He said to His disciples:

> "I will ask the Father, and he will give you another Helper, who will stay with you forever. He is the Spirit, who reveals the truth about God. The world cannot receive him, because it cannot see him or know him. But you know him, because he remains with you and is in you" (John 14:16–17).

MAN VS. GOD: THE ROOT OF ALL SPIRITUAL DISEASE

If the Christian belief system is truly beneficial to mental health, why do Christians ever need psychotherapy? If there existed a perfect Christian community populated by perfect Christian people (which in itself is an impossibility), psychotherapy might not be needed. It is far more likely, however, that such a need would still exist, for, as Christians believe, we live in a fallen world. The Bible makes it clear that there is an active force for evil at work in the world, and that this force is personified in Satan:

> Be alert, be on watch! Your enemy, the Devil, roams around like a roaring lion, looking for someone to devour (1 Pet. 5:8).

The Bible also states that good and evil exist coequally in all men:

> "There is no one who is righteous, no one who is wise or who worships God. All have turned away from God; they have all gone wrong; no one does what is right, not even one" (Rom. 3:10–12).

And it says that, at times, evil may even outweigh good to some degree. The apostle Paul is eloquent in his description of man's inherent warring nature:

> I know that good does not live in me—that is, in my human nature. For even though the desire to do good is in me, I am not able to do it. I don't do the good I want to do; instead, I do the evil that I do not want to do. . . . My inner being delights in the law of God. But I see a different law at work in my body—a law that fights against the law which my mind approves of. It makes me a prisoner to the law of sin which is at work in my body. What an unhappy man I am! Who will rescue me from this body that is taking me to death? Thanks be to God, who does this through our Lord Jesus Christ! (Rom. 7:18–19, 22–25).

Such beliefs contrast with those ideas held by the dynamicists and behavioralists, who view man as a blank entity
that is taught to be bad. The experientialists deny or mini-
mize man's evil or badness, and exalt instead his "innate
goodness." The Christian belief that man has within him an
inherent evil or fallen nature is the basis for the doctrine of
original sin.

Most Christian psychotherapists admit the existence of
sin and consider it to be a primary cause of man's spiritual
problems and many of his neuroses.

But what is sin?

Most persons think of sin as a specific type of negative
behavior, such as lying, stealing, cheating, murdering, or
being sexually promiscuous. Such actions are, to be sure,
manifestations of sin; but sin is more than specific negative
actions.

Sin is *conscious rebellion against the authority of God.*

Because of this natural tendency to rebel, man fails to
control his biological drives and chooses to relate to others
in ways that are contrary to the rules that God has given
him—rules that command that he relate to God and to
other people in *love.* Being alienated from God by his rebellion, man is not whole. His life becomes incomplete,
empty, and meaningless.

Sin has consequences that result in pathology or disease.
In his letter to the Romans, Paul goes so far as to say: "The
result of those things [referring to sin and all its ramifica-
tions] is death!" (Rom. 6:21). This biblical concept of
"death" has several interpretations. The most significant
aspect is alienation from God. Another is failure to receive
the abundant and eternal life that is promised to regenerate believers. Still another is the pain which results from
man's inability to control his behavior and from his failure
to respond to God's love. Pain is thus often the outgrowth
of evil. In his book, *The Problem of Pain,* C. S. Lewis has
pointed out:

Until the evil man finds evil unmistakably present in his existence in the form of pain, he is enclosed in an illusion. Once pain has roused him, he knows that he is in some way or another up against the real universe: He either rebels . . . or makes some attempt at adjustment which, if pursued, will lead him to religion.*

The painful emotions of sorrow, fear, anger, anxiety, emptiness, confusion, shame, jealousy, disgust, and guilt are all manifestations of spiritual pathology.

SALVATION: THE FIRST STEP TOWARD WHOLENESS

The concept of health usually considered to be characteristic of Christian psychotherapy is that of wholeness of "holiness." Tournier is a leading proponent of holiness in today's psychotherapeutic world—a world in which the word often conjures up images of emotional instability and religious fanaticism. But this is not what holiness originally meant. John Wesley, who was an outspoken proponent of holiness, believed that holiness (or sanctification) began with a transcendental experience (salvation through Christian conversion), but was at the outset incomplete. After salvation, the Christian life is one of constant self-inspection and striving toward improvement. It is in this context that I maintain salvation is not always enough for wholeness. It is, however, the all-important first step.

Wesley also believed that confession, reproof, instruction, and the performance of good works in love, were all part of the process through which behavior was modified and believers were made whole. In a world where medical care as we know it today was nonexistent, Wesley went to the trouble to write a book on home medical care. It is obvious that he did not omit the body in his concern for the

---

* C. S. Lewis, *The Problem of Pain* (New York: Macmillan; London: William Collins Sons & Co. Ltd, 1943). Used by permission.

whole man. Tournier's consideration of the whole man is in this same tradition.

THE HEALING POWER OF CHRISTIAN CONVERSION

While Christian psychotherapy employs many of the same techniques used in secular psychotherapy, it has as its primary goal for the patient, his or her *reconciliation with God through faith in Christ*—if this has not already taken place. A transcendental experience with God is one of the primary effectors of change.

Perhaps the key to understanding and accepting this phenomenon can be found in the words of Paul when he wrote to the church in Corinth: "When anyone is joined to Christ, he is a new being; the old is gone, the new has come." (2 Cor. 5:17). When a person becomes a believer, he receives a new and Holy Spirit; and with that Spirit, the potential to be wholly healed. As a physician and scientist, there was a time when I might have scoffed at such a concept. But as a believer, I've witnessed too many such healings to deny its validity.

WHY THE PAST IS IMPORTANT

In Christian therapy, as in many secular therapies, it is recognized that a patient's present reality is viewed through the past in anticipation of the future. For this reason, a full understanding of the patient's past is necessary to determine what changes must take place in order that new patterns of behavior can be established—patterns which are determined by the patient's Christian value system.

Christians cannot ignore the past any more than anyone else can, for in the past are buried the experiences—good and bad—that color their responses to the present and their attitudes toward the future. Christian therapists must, therefore, determine how the patient's past is influencing his present and his anticipation of the future. The intellectual and emotional knowledge gained in this way can then be used to help the patient better understand his current behavior. After the therapist and patient together have examined their findings in the light of the biblical ideal, it is then possible to initiate the necessary behavior modifications.

DURATION AND INTENSITY OF TREATMENT

Little has been written about the type and duration of treatment that Christian psychotherapists employ: long-term intense, long-term not intense, short-term intense, or short-term not intense. On the basis of my own experience and my understanding of the therapy employed by Tournier and others, I believe that any type is usable, and that the type is determined solely by the individual patient's need. After all, *the uniqueness of the individual* is a basic tenet of Christian belief. And it is conceptual narrowness of the worst kind to assume that all persons can be treated in the same manner.

BETWEEN THERAPIST AND PATIENT: A LOVE RELATIONSHIP

It could be said that the task of the Christian psychotherapist is more formidable than that of the strictly dynamic, behavioral, or experiential therapist, for he must be able to carry out the tasks of all three.

The therapist begins by establishing an atmosphere of mutual acceptance in order to encourage the patient's self-expression. To be effective in this task, the therapist must be a mature Christian who is able to interact with the patient in a nonjudgmental, loving way. He has to be able to accept the patient as he is and love him in spite of his problems. The love that the Christian therapist has must be the type of love that God has. This is known as divine or *agape* love. Such love is self-sacrificing; that is, it demands nothing and has as its primary concern the best interests and welfare of the other person. It is love that is nonsexual, nonexploitative, and long lasting. Such love is possible only if the therapist has, through conversion, already received God's Holy Spirit of love to amplify his own.

> Dear friends, let us love one another, because love comes from God. Whoever loves is a child of God and knows God. Whoever does not love does not know God, for God is love. And God showed his love for us by sending his only Son into the world, so that we might have life through him. . . . We love because God first loved us (1 John 4:7–9, 19).

The bond of love that is established between therapist and patient will of course be greater if both are Christians. At the beginning, the therapist must determine the nature of the patient's relationship with God and/or his level of maturity in the Christian faith. This demands a thorough knowledge of the Christian belief system.

D. E. Carlson, in his excellent analysis of Jesus' manner of relating to people as a model for counseling, described Him in roles that were *priestly, prophetic,* and *pastoral.* These roles correlate well with those employed by the three basic kinds of psychotherapies outlined by Karasu. The priestly, or all-knowing, authoritative role, is that which is typically assumed by the dynamic therapist and, to a lesser degree, by the behavioral therapist. The prophetic, or teaching, parental role, is that which is most assumed by the behavioral therapist. And the pastoral, or egalitarian, peer role, is that which is assumed by the experiential therapist.

Therapists of all kinds have an unfortunate tendency to assume the priestly or prophetic role with patients, while avoiding the pastoral one. Psychiatrists, psychologists, ministers, and other counselors often forget they are human. Yet their humanity is all too obvious, for there are more suicides, more problems with drug addiction and alcoholism, and as many divorces and problems with disturbed offspring among those employed in the so-called helping professions as there are in society at large.

With this in mind, it is noteworthy that the apostle Paul, in his letter to Titus, demands that leaders in the church be humble, mature persons whose lives reflect their wholeness as Christians.

> For since a church leader is in charge of God's work, he should be without fault. He must not be arrogant or quick-tempered, or a drunkard or violent or greedy for money. He must be hospitable and love what is good. He must be self-controlled, upright, holy, and disciplined. He must hold firmly to the message which can be trusted and which agrees with the doctrine. In this way he will be able to encourage others with the true teaching and also to show the error of those who are opposed to it (Titus 1:7–9).

Perhaps Paul recognized that it is all too easy for a leader who fails to recognize his own neurosis to pass it on to the very people he is trying to help. There are, therefore, times when the Christian therapist will be loving, accepting, and permissive. At other times, he will be dispassionate, confrontative, and frustrating. Each stance, however, is to be taken in love, with the patient's best interests in mind.

In his analysis, Carlson also notes that Jesus related to others in a wide variety of ways, most significantly as a critic, preacher, teacher, interpreter, mediator, confronter, admonisher, advocate, sustainer, lecturer, adviser, listener, reprover, warner, consoler, pardoner, supporter, helper, and burden-bearer. Most therapists today are committed to a single role model. Carlson, however, believes that the Christian therapist must be flexible, expanding his repertoire of counseling styles to include all of the ones listed above as the patient requires.

The Christian belief is that God loved the world so much that He sent His only Son to be a suffering servant for all humankind.

He always had the nature of God, but he did not think that by force he should try to become equal with God. Instead of this, of his own free will he gave up all he had, and took the nature of a servant. He became like man and appeared in human likeness. He was humble and walked the path of obedience all the way to death—his death on the cross. For this reason God raised him to the highest place above and gave him the name that is greater than any other name. And so, in honor of the name of Jesus all beings in heaven, on earth, and in the world below will fall on their knees, and all will openly proclaim that Jesus Christ is Lord, to the glory of God the Father (Phil. 2:6–11).

Within the counseling models listed by Carlson, the only ones that suggest the role of servant are those of supporter, helper, and burden-bearer. But Jesus' desire that all His followers are to be one in love removes any notion that their relationship with one another should be anything but egalitarian. Humility is a quality that grows, in part, out of love for one's fellow persons.

The relationship of the Christian therapist to his patient is, therefore, one of loving acceptance. The therapist does not conceive of himself as a priest with special virtues or with special access to God. He recognizes that he is not superior and has, himself, no unusual ability to handle conflict. He is, however, a person who has been given gifts of knowledge and healing which he is to use to help humankind in a harsh world. The Christian therapist and his patients are fellow strugglers. Their relationship is genuine as they both depend and draw upon the same source for guidance and strength—God.

THE CHRISTIAN THERAPIST'S TOOLS AND TECHNIQUES

The primary tools and techniques of the Christian psychotherapist are those used by dynamic, behavioral, and experiential psychotherapists—with several important additions.

Once the appropriate atmosphere has been established and the therapist has determined the level at which he and the patient are to relate, he must explore the patient's areas of conflict and their origins. In many cases, it will be necessary to strip away the defenses by which the patient maintains repression of the experiences that have given rise to his symptoms.

Christians are particularly prone to deny conflict, simply because it is not compatible with their (misguided) notion of Christian perfection. Having been taught (quite wrongly) that Christians *"never* get angry, *never* think lustful thoughts, *never* fornicate or commit adultery, and *always* love,"* the patient who considers himself a Christian may deny or repress any "un-Christian" feelings or behavior. The therapist must be familiar with these defenses and know how to get around them so that he can comprehend the patient's unconscious mental conflict and its historical and hidden meanings.

Next, the therapist has the task of helping the patient understand how this unconscious conflict is influencing his current behavior. By responding to the patient in ways that do not reward the behaviors that produce pain and anxiety, the therapist helps to bring about extinction or inhibition of such behaviors. He then must teach or program new behavioral patterns that will provide the patient with appropriate positive reinforcements. Since the Christian therapist will use biblical guidelines in his selection of the new behaviors, familiarity with the Bible is essential. The use of psychodrama, visualization techniques, or role-playing often helps the patient to get in touch with his long-repressed feelings, so that he can take some definitive action to deal with them.

Of particular importance is the management of anger. In many cases, a patient's symptoms or behavioral aberrations are derived from hate, resentment, or what the Bible refers to as "record of wrongs" (1 Cor. 13:5) that people tend to hold against each other. The only effective way to deal with these records of wrongs is to call upon God's *forgiveness,* but modern psychology seems to have no place in its scheme for such a concept. Dynamic psychologists believe that simple understanding or insight results in forgiveness; behavioralists, since they do not believe that there is responsibility, see no necessity for forgiveness; experientialists regard man as inherently good, and therefore do not even consider the need for forgiveness. For the Christian, however, it is impossible to deny that moral responsibility exists. When an individual has broken one of God's laws, he is guilty of transgression and must deal with the resulting guilt.

Most Christian therapists emphasize the role of forgiveness in Christian psychotherapy. Biblically, God is the source of all forgiveness—for forgiveness can come only out of the infinite love He has for humankind. It is the task of the therapist to help his patient call upon this forgiveness in order to deal with the anger he has toward others, and also with the anger and shame he feels about his own behavior. Once the patient has accepted God's forgiveness for himself and for those who he feels have wronged him, he can relate to others in love, and can develop a realistic self-concept.

By far the most vital tool available to the Christian psychotherapist is *conversion.* Biblically based Christian therapy takes seriously the statement of Jesus, "No one can see the Kingdom of God unless he is born again" (John 3:3). Spiritual regeneration through conversion is the *sine qua non*—the essential element—of truly Christian therapy.

Wholeness cannot be attained without it. Even nonbe-
lievers attest to the importance and usefulness of conversion in some healings—especially alcoholism. In fact, it is
the spiritual dimension at the heart of Alcoholics Anonymous that is credited for this organization's amazing success. To illustrate, consider the following first three steps
of A. A.'s famous "Twelve Steps" method:

1. We admitted we were powerless over alcohol—that our
lives had become unmanageable.
2. Came to believe that a Power greater than ourselves
could restore us to sanity.
3. Made a decision to turn our will and our lives over to the
care of God as we understood him. . . .

Yet another unique tool available to the Christian therapist is a *reward system* that produces a highly motivated
patient. For the Christian, there is the promise of the fruit
of the Holy Spirit: "love, joy, peace, patience, kindness,
goodness, faithfulness, humility, and self-control" (Gal.
5:22–23). There are also the promises of abundant and eternal life:

"I have come in order that you might have life—life in all its
fullness" (John 10:10).

For God loved the world so much that he gave his only Son,
so that everyone who believes in him may not die but have
eternal life (John 3:16).

All of these promises serve as powerful incentives for
working toward healing.

The Christian therapist can also utilize *prayer, Bible
study,* and *worship* to help him in his teaching and condi-
tioning task. A fine example of the therapeutic use of
prayer is illustrated by Norman Grubb's theory that prayer
is intended not to convince God of a need for change, but to
convince the suppliant. The *Eucharist,* properly under-

stood, is also a powerful tool for bringing about both spiritual renewal and healing.

CONCLUSION

Christian psychotherapy is more than secular psychotherapy carried out by a Christian therapist in a Christian environment. As emphasized earlier in this book, Christian psychotherapy is based on the premise that the prime mover of the universe is a personal God who has revealed Himself to humankind through the Person of His Son, Jesus Christ, and through His Word, the Bible, and who is also capable of indwelling a person through His Holy Spirit.

The key to healing in Christian psychotherapy is, initially, the patient's reconciliation to God through a regenerate faith in Christ. Through conversion, a patient receives God's indwelling Holy Spirit—a very personal counselor, comforter, and source of healing power. In addition, he is also given the potential for no less than an entirely new personality.

Drawing upon this transforming and healing power of the Holy Spirit, the Christian psychotherapist works to cleanse the patient of painful emotions and undesirable behavior patterns. He has at his employ a wide variety of therapeutic methods and techniques, including such particularly Christian tools such as conversion, prayer, forgiveness, and the Eucharist. He encourages in the patient the adoption of new behavior and values, biblically based, that will serve to make a favorable difference in the patient's life. As motivation, he offers the patient hope for a future that promises abundant life on this earth, as well as eternal life after death.

Continued healing and growth take place not only through the efforts of the Christian therapist, but also through the patient's acceptance by and involvement with a local Christian community, including religious instruction and corpo-

rate worship, and through the individual's prayer life and
study of God's Word, as revealed through the Bible.

A WORD FOR THERAPISTS

Christian therapy has been available since Pentecost, for
it was at that time nearly two-thousand years ago that the
personalities of the disciples were dramatically changed
when they were filled with the Holy Spirit. (This is re-
corded in detail in the second chapter of the Book of Acts.)
The truth revealed in the New Testament provides guidelines for the continued therapy of all believers after their
conversion. Modern secular techniques offer only frag-
ments of the truth revealed in the Bible, because their
primary concern is not for the whole person, but for some
limited dimension of his life.

For the therapist who does not believe in a personal God,
the use of conversion, prayer, and forgiveness as therapeutic tools may seem foolish, and the belief that a Holy Spirit
can dwell in a person and be an agent of change may appear
absurd. If the patient holds these beliefs, however, the
therapist would be wise to use them in his treatment rather
than ignore or attack them. The person who has been spiritually regenerated through belief in Christ has a faith that
must be accepted and utilized if therapy is to be successful,
for he is not likely to give it up.

The therapist also has to recognize that some of the patient's conflicts may arise out of his faith and its practice.
Many Christian patients have problems stemming from a
misinterpretation of biblical principles, or an overemphasis
on certain aspects of Christian values, beliefs, or experience. To condemn the beliefs of a Christian patient, unless
they are glaringly in error and/or are contributing to his
problems, will only hinder therapy by increasing the patient's anxiety. It is imperative, therefore, that a Christian
therapist have a good understanding of theology and of the

beliefs held by different branches of the Christian faith. *When a Christian therapist adheres too rigidly to a strictly dispensationalist, pentecostal, or fundamentalist view of the Bible, he may create some of the same problems caused by secular therapy.*

In no uncertain terms, Jesus has referred to the Holy Spirit as the exclusive agent "who reveals the truth about God" (John 14:17). For this reason, it is necessary that both patient and therapist clearly understand the work and Person of the Holy Spirit. Without this knowledge, progress may be slow.

Finally, Christian psychotherapists should, without fail, utilize prayer as their primary therapeutic technique. Prayer is a conversation between two beings who love one another—God and man. The members of the therapeutic trio—God, patient, and therapist—have to be in communication if therapy is to be effective. Praying *with* a patient as well as for him, often opens the way to a closer and more honest relationship between two people who love God and are seeking His help.

The results of Christian psychotherapy—as the following case histories illustrate—are often amazing.

PART III

TOUCHED
BY
GOD'S
LOVE

Five Lives Made New

Introduction

As I have stressed earlier, salvation alone is not always enough for healing. It is, however, the essential first step. In the course of my career, I have treated literally thousands of patients. The following five individuals have been singled out to appear in this book because not only do their stories vividly illustrate when and why salvation is not enough, they also provide excellent insight into these five basic principles of Christian psychotherapy:

1. How Christianity Builds Self-Esteem
2. The Healing Power of the Christian Community
3. The Healing Power of the Eucharist
4. The Healing Power of Repentance, Confession, and Forgiveness
5. The Centrality of Christ as It Relates to Healing

It is important for the reader to understand that each of the men and women represented here suffered illnesses which did not respond to the most advanced medicine and treatments that secular medicine had to offer. Something more was necessary for these five people to achieve wholeness. And that something more was no less than the healing touch of God's love.

In the Book of Jeremiah in the Old Testament, the prophet evokes the Lord's plaintive cry for the fate of His children who, for various reasons, cannot or will not be healed: "Is there no medicine in Gilead? Are there no doctors there?" (Jer. 8:22).

It is my belief that thanks to the healing power of God's love as experienced through applied Christian psychotherapy, we can at last respond affirmatively, "Yes, Lord, there is medicine! Yes, Lord, there are doctors!"

The lives of the following five men and women offer glorious testimony to the good news of wholeness through Christ.

1

PETER

How Christianity Builds
Self-Esteem

As Jesus was walking along, he saw a man who had been born blind. His disciples asked him, "Teacher, whose sin caused him to be born blind? Was it his own or his parents' sin?"

Jesus answered, "His blindness has nothing to do with his sins or his parents' sins. He is blind so that God's power might be seen at work in him" (John 9:1-3).

One day a young woman named Jenny approached me to ask if her husband, Peter, could make an appointment to see me. Peter was severely visually impaired. According to Jenny, two months earlier Peter had heard me speak at a Lay Witness Mission at their church. He had been so intrigued by the first night's proceedings that he had gone on to attend every session. As the weekend passed, he heard many people tell how Christ had changed their lives, and how Christ could do the same for him, as well. For several months, added Jenny, Peter had been longing to believe, but this was the first time that anyone had ever told him how. By the time the Sunday morning worship service took place and the invitation was extended, Peter was convinced. One of the first to respond, he approached the communion rail and surrendered his life to Christ.

Still, Peter had many problems. Because I was a psychiatrist who was also a Christian, he hoped that I might be able to help him.

I told Jenny that I would be happy to meet with her husband, and we set up an appointment for early the next week.

Peter was a well-built man, about five-feet, ten-inches tall, and in his early thirties. From a small town, his manner was simple and unassuming. Legally blind, he wore one-half-inch-thick glasses which made his bright blue eyes appear unnaturally small. But as Peter began to tell me about his life, it was clear that his poor vision was just one of many problems.

Born nearly totally blind, Peter's vision was so impaired that even with corrective lenses, he could distinguish only shadows in one eye, and barely see to make his way around with the other.

Raised in the poorest section of a small mill town, no one disciplined Peter as a child because of his infirmity. "I was petted and humored, and nobody held me accountable for anything," he told me. His way of avoiding responsibility was to throw a temper tantrum. Once in a while his father would try to intervene with disciplinary measures, but when this happened, Peter's soft-hearted mother would step in and countermand her husband's efforts.

When Peter entered the first grade, he was unable to see clearly the standard-sized print used in school books, and therefore failed to learn to read. Why Peter wasn't sent to the State School for the Blind, he did not know. For the next six years, throughout elementary school, he tried his best to learn to read, but without success. When he finally did obtain a book with large enough print, he saw the words "backwards," which indicated to me that he also may have a mild form of dyslexia.

"In my whole life," said Peter, "I've owned only three books that have had print large enough for me to see." He expressed shame and resentment for his near illiteracy and his parents' failure to obtain professional help for his problem.

As Peter grew older, he recognized that because of his impaired eyesight he could not compete with other boys in many of their activities—scholastic or athletic. When he was ten years old, in an effort to bolster his extremely low sense of self-esteem, he began to steal. At first, Peter stole from five-and-dime stores, and only small items such as pencils, erasers, candy bars, and gum. But in later years he developed a preference for hardware stores, and began stealing larger items such as screwdrivers, lightbulbs, saws, and hammers. Even with his poor vision, Peter became something of an expert at pilfering—especially flat objects, which he slipped under his sweater, up his sleeve, or concealed with a loosely held coat. Because this compulsive stealing was a habit Peter had never overcome, and something he had never confessed to anyone, it was with great difficulty that he admitted it to me.

In time, Peter quit school and eventually obtained a job in a large university's botany department, where he was responsible for watering and feeding plants in a phytotron. (A phytotron is a huge greenhouse where many varieties of plants, including full-size trees, are grown and studied under controlled environmental conditions.) It was about this time when Peter met and later married Jenny.

Once married, it would seem that Peter had at last adjusted to life. Still, he continued to have problems. Subject to periods of depression, he was hospitalized on several occasions. At another time, he and Jenny sought counseling because of marital problems. Basically, Peter's problems stemmed from his infantile behavior. As a result of his undisciplined upbringing, he was selfish, self-centered, and emotionally uncontrolled. Both at home and on the job, he was subject to uncontrollable outbursts of temper, and if he couldn't have his own way in matters, he would sulk for days. Even Peter acknowledged that Jenny spent far too much of her time placating him.

About a year and a half before his first session with me, Peter had begun attending church. At the same time, he had enrolled in a special reading clinic. As a result, his reading skills improved—but not as much as Peter might have liked.

Upon becoming a Christian, Peter believed it was imperative that his negative and destructive behavior patterns somehow be changed. He was most bothered by his compulsive stealing. As Peter had been stealing regularly from two hardware stores for more than two years, he had stashed away in his garage several large cardboard boxes full of stolen (and never-used) goods. The approximate value of the cache was nearly two thousand dollars!

"Please, Dr. Wilson," Peter pleaded at the close of our first session. "Help me." His tiny blue eyes registered fear and deep humiliation.

I should mention here that the medical term for compulsive stealing such as Peter's is *kleptomania*. Like the compulsive gambler and those who suffer compulsive sexual perversions such as exhibitionism or fetishism, the kleptomaniac obtains a certain sense of satisfaction from his act of stealing. Typically, kleptomania is caused by a deep sense of inadequacy and inferiority. To steal makes the person feel temporarily significant. A psychologically determined neurosis, kleptomania nearly always requires professional treatment, and even then is extremely difficult to cure.

During Peter's sessions with me for the next several weeks, we talked about his kleptomania at length. Employing a Christian perspective, we discussed in depth the nature and reality of sin, and how Peter's compulsive stealing was—in a very real way—an example of sinful behavior. We talked about the destructive toll that sin takes on a person's life, and again looked to Peter's current unhappiness as a good example of this. In addition, we explored the reasons behind Peter's willful sinning through stealing: He stole because he had a need to; because it brought him some sort of satisfaction; and because it made him feel—if only for a moment—that he was important.

We also discussed the only means by which Peter could

truly rid himself of his sinful behavior and its accompanying guilt. He would have to (1) *repent* of his sin (to repent literally means to "turn around," or change); (2) *confess* his sin to God (and to others if necessary); (3) *ask for and accept God's forgiveness;* and (4) make a special effort from that point on to *never steal again.*

It was during Peter's fifth session that he suddenly announced he couldn't stand it any longer—he had to get rid of his cache of stolen merchandise. The presence of the goods in his garage was a source of unbearable guilt and anxiety. "But how do you think I should go about returning everything?" he asked.

"Well," I replied, "you've got several alternatives. First, you could simply take the merchandise back, confess your misdeeds to the store managers, ask for their forgiveness, and accept the consequences—whatever they may be. A second possibility might be to somehow return the goods with an anonymous confessional note. Your third alternative is simply to do nothing."

Peter said that he would think it over.

He showed up in my office the following week to announce that he had decided to return the stolen property personally, ask for the store owners' forgiveness, and accept the consequences.

I have always wished that I had volunteered to accompany Peter when he returned his boxes of stolen goods. How I would like to have seen the faces of each of those store managers when a blind man, pushing a dolly laden with boxes of merchandise, entered their store only to confess that he had stolen the items from them over the past two years!

As Peter told me later, his heart was pounding as he pushed open the door to the first hardware store. For a moment, he wanted to turn and flee. When the manager asked him what he wanted, this is what he said: "All my life I've felt inferior. Because of this, I stole these things to make me feel better. I'm sorry. I know what I did was

wrong. I want to return your merchandise. I want you to
know that I will never steal from you again. If you would
prefer that I never again return to your store, I won't. I'm
just hoping that you will forgive me." In both instances the
managers forgave Peter, and asked him to feel free to return to their stores any time he wanted, at the same time
assuring him that they would be pleased to have him as
their customer.

Because of this positive experience, Peter felt a lot less
guilty. Still, he said he felt as though he needed something
more in order to feel fully healed of his need to steal.

From our very first session together, I had used a
lovingly confrontative approach with Peter. Because of the
little discipline he had received while growing up, he
needed someone who would relate to him firmly and with
some degree of authority.

"Peter," I said, when he told me he still experienced a
sense of guilt, "you realize that when you stole, what you
did was wrong, correct?"

"Yes," he replied. "I realize what I did was wrong."

"And you know that while I don't approve of your stealing, when you confessed it to me, I forgave you, correct?"

"That's right."

"And you know that while the store managers from
whom you stole didn't approve of your stealing, when you
confessed your behavior to them, they forgave you, too,
correct?"

"That's right."

"Well then, I guess you also know that the one Person
who also disapproves of your stealing and who is still awaiting your confession is God, wouldn't you agree?"

Peter said nothing.

"Peter," I said quietly, "through the Bible, God has told
us that if we confess our sins to Him, He will keep His
promise and forgive us. Do you understand that when you
confess your stealing to God, He will forgive you? And by
forgive, I mean that He will *forget* your sin. As far as east
is from west, He says He will remove your sin from you."

Still, Peter said nothing.

"Peter," I persisted, "if *I* can forgive you—and if those two *store managers* can forgive you—think how much more able *God*, who is our perfect Father in heaven, can forgive you!"

Suddenly it was as though sunlight broke through in Peter's eyes as he grasped what I had been trying to tell him about the fullness of God's forgiveness.

"You're right!" he exclaimed. "I see what you mean!"

"Well, good," I said. "Now that you understand the magnitude of God's forgiveness, I think it's time you took a few moments for some good prayer. You can pray with me now, if you like, or you can pray later when you get home. Either way, tell God that you know what you've done is wrong. Tell Him that you're sorry and you want to change. Tell Him that you recognize that He is faithful to His word and will forgive you. Tell Him that you will accept His forgiveness. And tell Him that you're trusting that He will help you to never steal again."

"I'd like to pray now," said Peter. "With you."

And that's exactly what he did.

Since that day, Peter has never stolen again. His kleptomania is cured.

Still, there remained in Peter's life several other problems to be dealt with, most notably his continuing emotional problems and poor reading skills.

One day, while discussing his reading, I asked Peter if he had ever tried reading the Bible.

"I don't own one with print large enough for reading," he replied.

I happened to have in my desk drawer a big-print edition of *Good News for Modern Man*, which had been given to me by one of my patients. Handing the book to Peter, I asked him if he could read it. Walking over to the window, Peter held the book about six inches from his eyes, and—for the first time in his life—read from the Bible. His response to the experience was utter elation!

In ensuing months I spent considerable time working

with Peter on his problems of low self-esteem and emotional sensitivity. Because he tended to be discouraged easily, progress was slow—but steady. In time, Peter's mood swings and supersensitivity decreased, and he became more satisfied with his life. It was then that I turned him over to a colleague for additional marital counseling.

A full year passed before I saw Peter again. I had been asked to lead a Lay Witness Mission in a church in suburban Washington, D.C., and was in the process of selecting members for my team. Recalling how Peter had once offered his services in this regard, I phoned him to ask if he might like to join us. He accepted eagerly. When he arrived at my home on an early Friday morning for the six-hour drive to our destination, his enthusiasm for the coming weekend was obvious.

It wasn't until we arrived at the church and began to meet with members of the congregation that I began to realize the highly intellectual nature of the group. Because of the church's location, many members were high-level government employees—most of whom worked at the National Institute of Health and other scientific institutions in the area. Nearly everyone was a college graduate, and a large percentage had their master's or doctoral degrees. In addition, there were many lawyers and physicians.

Fortunately, our mission team of laymen was appropriately matched. Among us there were several physicians, lawyers, engineers, and educators. Peter, with his grammar school education, was the one exception.

It was for this reason that I began to have serious doubts about the wisdom of my inviting Peter on this particular Mission. Peter, after all, was barely capable of reading. What effect could a simple person like him possibly have on such an intellectual group? As the weekend progressed, I found myself deliberately avoiding calling upon Peter to share his testimony. While I felt vaguely guilty about this, I was glad to observe that Peter's enthusiasm for the Mission seemed not dampened in the least.

On Sunday morning, prior to the eleven o'clock worship service and noon luncheon that would mark the close of the Mission weekend, I assigned two or three team members to each of the various Sunday school classes. Peter was assigned to the adult class. Although this was a class that included many highly educated individuals, the Mission was so close to over that I was no longer concerned about Peter's possible negative effect.

How mistaken I was to have been worried at all!

Later, at the closing luncheon, I was approached by several members of the Adult class to which Peter had been assigned—all of whom had glowing reports of Peter's contribution to the class.

"Bill," said one, "you should have been there. I've never been so moved as when I heard the testimony by that young man with the poor eyesight." Said another, "I don't know that I'll ever be the same after hearing that man named Peter. What a shame everyone couldn't have heard him!"

From what I gathered from those who were there—and from Peter himself, who told me about it later during the ride home—this is what happened:

After the Sunday school leader made a brief introductory statement, he called upon Peter to share his testimony. With the same enthusiasm he had maintained all weekend, Peter got up, walked to the front of the classroom, and told the group about being born blind. He spoke frankly about the difficulties of his early life, his resulting psychiatric problems, and his inability to read. He then went on to tell how he had been spiritually regenerated upon accepting Christ during a Lay Witness Mission that had taken place at his church. He told how his fellow churchmen had helped him with his reading, and how he had obtained his first large-print Bible.

Then, opening his Bible to the Book of Ephesians, Peter announced that he was going to read from the Scriptures. Raising the book to his usual reading position—six inches from his bespectacled eyes—Peter placed his index finger under the first word and began to read. Slowly and laboriously, not unlike a first or second grade student, he shared this message:

> I ask God from the wealth of his glory to give you power through his Spirit to be strong in your inner selves, and I pray that Christ will make his home in your hearts through faith. I pray that you may have your roots and foundation in love, so that you, together with all God's people, may have the power to understand how broad and long, how high and deep, is Christ's love. Yes, may you come to know his love—although it can never be fully known—and so be completely filled with the very nature of God (Eph. 3:16–19).

It would be impossible for me to describe the effect that Peter's reading had on his audience. From what I was told, there was not a dry eye in the room. Here, after all, was a simple man, delightedly reading from one of the few readable books he had ever owned to an assemblage of persons who could rightly be called intellectuals. While reading about the unsearchable depth of God's love, Peter—healed and whole through faith in Jesus—was a living testimony to the truth of what he was reading, and everyone in the room knew it. Even the most hardened skeptic was hard put to deny the reality and power of God's love after meeting Peter.

In retrospect I, perhaps as much as anyone, am grateful for knowing Peter. This is because he has helped me to understand far more fully not only the depth of God's love, but the nature of what God considers to be true wisdom, true power, and true strength—qualities which God and humans perceive very differently.

> For what seems to be God's foolishness is wiser than human wisdom, and what seems to be God's weakness is stronger than human strength (1 Cor. 1:25).

*   *   *

In light of applied Christian psychotherapy, Peter's case provides an excellent example of how faith in God, including a full understanding of the forgiving and unconditional nature of God's love through Christ, enables a person—even one so troubled as Peter—to realize he is a worthwhile person.

Self-esteem is determined largely by how an individual is loved and accepted (or perceives that he is loved and accepted) by his parents and, to a lesser degree, by his peers. While Peter's parents may in fact have loved him very much, their failure to discipline him and to seek help for his eye problem when he was growing up, indicated otherwise. In addition, Peter was alternately ostracized and ignored by his peers, and this further exacerbated his already dangerously low sense of self-esteem. It was in his desperate attempt to gain some sense of significance and purpose that Peter finally resorted to stealing.

Jesus often stressed the necessity of "loving oneself"—a phrase which implies having a realistic self-concept and healthy sense of self-worth. He even went so far as to teach what is now a generally accepted psychological verity: that a person is capable of loving others only so far as he is able to love himself.

> We love because God first loved us (1 John 4:19).

> "'Love the Lord your God with all your heart, with all your soul, and with all your mind.' This is the greatest and the most important commandment. The second most important commandment is like it: 'Love your neighbor as you love yourself'" (Matt. 22:37–39).

But how does a person learn to love himself?

For individuals like Peter, who suffer extremely low self-esteem, it has been my observation that conversion to Christianity can make all the difference. Basically this is because of the realistic self-concept that Christianity requires. For the believer, this realistic appraisal of self includes first the understanding that he is a sinner; that is, as a human being he possesses a fallen, unholy spirit, and is therefore naturally separated from God. At the same time, the believer understands that he has been saved from his sinfulness by the redemptive death of Jesus Christ on the cross, and that he is empowered to experience wholeness through the indwelling presence of Christ's Holy Spirit. The regenerate believer also understands that he is forever forgiven and unconditionally loved by God the Father—a Father who values the personhood of each of His children so much that He sent His only Son, Jesus, to die for them. Through Jesus, the believer becomes a "child of God" in the very truest sense of the phrase.

To know that he is so fully loved by God provides the Christian with a rock-solid sense of self that cannot be obtained through any other source—not through parents, mates, children, or friends. The constancy and magnitude of God's love, and the infiniteness of His mercy as expressed through the Person and life of Christ, not only serve to enhance the believer's sense of self-esteem, but also provide him with a meaningful and purposeful life.

2

ROSE

The Healing Power of the Christian Community

The teachers of the Law and the Pharisees brought in a woman who had been caught committing adultery, and they made her stand before them all. "Teacher," they said to Jesus, "this woman was caught in the very act of committing adultery. In our Law Moses commanded that such a woman must be stoned to death. Now, what do you say?" They said this to trap Jesus, so that they could accuse him. But he bent over and wrote on the ground with his finger. As they stood there asking him questions, he straightened up and said to them, "Whichever one of you has committed no sin may throw the first stone at her." Then he bent over again and wrote on the ground. When they heard this, they all left, one by one, the older ones first. Jesus was left alone with the woman still standing there. He straightened up and said to her, "Where are they? Is there no one left to condemn you?"

"No one, sir," she answered.

"Well then," Jesus said, "I do not condemn you either. Go, but do not sin again" (John 8:3–11).

It was not under the best of circumstances that I first met Rose. A young prostitute, she had been admitted to the hospital after attempting suicide through a drug overdose—her eighth attempt over the past several months.

115

Earlier in the year, when Rose had been admitted to the hospital for one of her previous suicide attempts, she had remained hospitalized for four months, running up a bill of nearly six thousand dollars, which she had been unable to pay. Now, because of Rose's lack of funds, her regular doctor had refused to take her on again as his patient. It was only because I happened to be the doctor on call at the time of Rose's admittance to the hospital that she was now my responsibility. To further complicate matters, I had been notified by the hospital's business office that because of Rose's bad financial situation, it would be necessary for me to arrange for her transfer to the State Hospital as soon as possible. (The State Hospital charges patients only as much as they are able to pay.) Should Rose refuse to be transferred voluntarily, it would then be my unpleasant task to legally commit her.

It was, therefore, with something of a chip on my shoulder that I entered Rose's room to introduce myself and to inform her of these matters.

Rose was in her early twenties, tall, large-boned, and plump. Her demeanor and attire were what one might expect of a woman of the streets. Her limp brown hair was parted in the middle and fell down over her shoulders. Her slacks were so tight that they fit her ample form like a second skin. She wore an ultra-sheer blouse, suggestively unbuttoned and tied around her midriff in a large knot. She regarded me apprehensively with pale green eyes.

Rather brusquely, I introduced myself and explained to Rose that I was to be her doctor only so long as she was a patient at this hospital. In an equally matter-of-fact tone, I went on to inform her that because of her lack of money it would be necessary for her to be transferred to the State Hospital as soon as possible, whether such a move was agreeable to her or not.

I waited for Rose's response, but she said nothing. I noticed, however, a flicker of fear behind her eyes. I left her room with the promise that I would be returning in two days to discuss the matter with her more fully.

The next morning, I was shocked to learn that on the previous night, just a few hours after I had spoken to her, Rose had again attempted suicide—this time using old prescribed antidepressant drugs that she had somehow smuggled onto the ward. One of the attending psychiatric aides, a woman named Pickett, told me that Rose said she had tried to kill herself because she didn't want to be transferred to the State Hospital.

Wondering why Rose would be so upset about changing hospitals, I pulled her chart. As I reviewed her history, I quickly discovered the origin of her fear.

Born illegitimately, Rose was not placed for adoption through a legal agency, but bootlegged into a chaotic home where alcoholic foster parents hoped that a child might help save their floundering marriage. Unfortunately, Rose only became a victim of their unhappiness. Throughout her childhood, she was both emotionally and physically abused.

The most severe abuse suffered by Rose took place when she was eight years old and was sexually used by her sixteen-year-old foster brother. Now it is a fact that children cannot deal with sexual stimulation so early in life, and therefore not surprising that soon after puberty Rose found herself entangled in repeated sexual difficulties. She was regularly abused by her foster brother until her early teens, by which time she had also become involved in sexual activities with other youngsters in the neighborhood. At age fourteen, Rose either seduced or was seduced by a male high school teacher, and was caught with him in the sexual act. Because Rose could offer no excuse for her behavior that her foster parents could accept, they angrily committed her to the State Hospital as an incorrigible sexual psychopath. For the next four years of her life—a time when most young women are caught up with school, dating, football games, and proms—Rose languished in a psychiatric ward in the company of thirty chronically mentally ill women. Her schooling was abandoned and, because she received few visitors, her social skills all but disappeared.

Most tragic of all was the inappropriate treatment that

Rose received at the State Hospital. Instead of being surrounded by hardened psychotics, what she needed was a nurturing environment—perhaps another foster home—where she would have been loved and cared for, and able to receive appropriate counseling. No wonder Rose preferred to take her life rather than return to the State Hospital!

At the legal age of eighteen, Rose was released from the State Hospital "on her own recognizance." But where was she to go? What was she to do? Her foster family wanted nothing to do with her; she had no education, no marketable skills. Rose was forced, therefore, to sell the only thing she had—her body.

Although upon direct questioning Rose denied that she was a prostitute, she did admit that the next two years of her life were spent on the street, and that casual sexual activity was a regular part of her existence. When she was twenty years old, she married an itinerant worker some thirty years her senior. From the day they were married, Rose's husband encouraged her to engage in sex with younger men because he thought she "would enjoy them more." Because her husband was gone most of the time, Rose did find other partners and in a short time became pregnant by one of them. About a year after her marriage, Rose gave birth to a baby boy. Shortly after the baby was born, it was discovered that he suffered a crippling birth defect.

When her son was three years old, Rose separated from her husband to move in with a boyfriend—but because the man physically abused her, this arrangement, too, fell apart. It was about this time that Rose sat down and contemplated her life. In utter despair, she realized that she had nothing to look back upon and nothing to look forward to. Because her life made no sense—had no meaning—she decided to end it all.

Four times Rose almost succeeded in killing herself. It was her eighth attempt that had brought her to me. Now I had the dubious distinction of having provided the cause for her ninth attempt.

Though I now understood Rose's fear of returning to the State Hospital, I still had no choice but to proceed with her transfer as originally planned. Upon notifying the State Hospital of Rose's situation, I was informed that they would be able to receive her as soon as I could arrange either a voluntary or legal commitment. Now, all that was left for me to do was to persuade Rose to transfer—an obviously difficult task.

It was with grim determination that I approached Rose's room to present her with an ultimatum: either she would agree to be transferred to the State Hospital voluntarily, or I would be forced to commit her. At the same time I told her how after reading her chart I understood her reluctance to return to a place which contained for her such unhappy memories. Leaving her with instructions to think the matter over, I said that I would return the following day to learn what she had decided.

Late the next morning I headed for the psychiatric ward for my meeting with Rose. Accompanying me was a young doctor named Russ Kilpatrick, who had just graduated from medical school and who had asked if he might observe me on my rounds. Upon entering Rose's room, we found her sitting cross-legged on her bed, deep in conversation with Pickett, the psychiatric aide who had helped her through her most recent suicide attempt.

Now, to fully explain the dynamics at work in Rose's story, I must digress for a moment to share a bit about Pickett—a woman whose story is worth hearing in its own right.

Tall and skinny, with laughing dark eyes and a quick wit, Pickett had worked as an aide on our ward for nearly as long as I could remember. I'd always liked the woman, although she did have one nasty habit: Pickett was a chronic curser. Now this was a trait that had never bothered me before I was a believer; after all, at one time my own language had been equally atrocious. After I became a Christian, however, Pickett's profanity drove me batty.

One day, while the two of us were engaged in conversation in the nurses' station, Pickett cut loose with a string of curse words that threatened to turn the air blue. It wasn't that Pickett was upset or angry; profanity was simply a part of her vocabulary. Finally, I could put up with it no longer.

"Pickett," I interrupted, "you know I love you, but for a long time now there's been something I've wanted to tell you. Your foul mouth drives me up the wall. I sure do wish there was something you could do about it."

Her response took me by surprise.

"I wish there was, too," she said. "It's a damn nasty habit, and I'd give anything to get rid of it."

For a moment I was silent, recalling how one of the first effects of my conversion was that I had stopped cursing. Then, impulsively, I said, "You know, Pickett, there is something you can do about it."

"What do you mean?" she asked.

Not wanting to tell her about Jesus right there in the middle of the nurses' station, I suggested that we move to the treatment room across the hall.

"Fine," agreed Pickett. "You lead the way."

Together the two of us crossed the hall to the treatment room where, against the unlikely setting of therapeutic instruments and machines, I told Pickett about my conversion experience, and how believing in Jesus and in His Holy Spirit had so totally transformed my life—especially my old habit of swearing. Through the grace of God, I must have said the right thing at the right time, because Pickett responded to my words with obvious interest. Before we left the treatment room she prayed for Jesus to enter and change her life, and from that day on I never heard her curse again.

In passing months, Pickett and I often found time to pray together; many times it was for her brother, who was suffering from a terminal illness. It was with a sense of joy and wonder that I watched as Pickett's faith grew—daily it seemed—as did her understanding of the healing power of God's love.

This was the Pickett who had befriended Rose, and who now looked up to greet Russ and me as we entered the room.

"Dr. Wilson!" she exclaimed. "You're just the man we were hoping to see. Rose has something she wants to tell you."

"What is it?" I asked.

I noticed that Rose was holding a purple memo pad, the pages of which were cleaved in the middle and rounded at the top—not unlike the tablets of the Law that Moses is traditionally portrayed as holding.

Lowering her eyes, Rose handed the memo pad to me. On the right-hand side, written in a child-like script, was this letter:

"Heavenly Father," I read quietly, "is there no one in the world who will come and tell me about you? Please, dear God, send someone to tell me about you. Love, Rose."

Tears welled up in my eyes as I choked out my response.

"Rose," I said, "do you have any idea who this heavenly Father is that you've written to?"

"No," she replied, "but you do. Pickett says you do. I believe her, and I believe that you are the one who is going to tell me all about God."

I glanced at Pickett, who—like Russ and myself—was doing her best not to cry.

For the next hour and a half, I shared with Rose everything I knew about God's love for all humankind and, specifically, about His special love for her. I explained to Rose that even if she had been the only person in the whole world, God still would have sent Jesus to die for her sins. I told her how because of His great love for her, she could be forgiven and cleansed; and how through the help of His Holy Spirit living in her, she could be empowered to become a new person. I explained that if only she could find it in her heart to trust in God, He would look after her and meet her every need. I then went on to tell Rose about my conversion experience and the tremendous effect that it had had on my own life.

"Rose," I said when I had finished, "would you like to know Jesus as your Lord and Savior?"

"Oh, yes," she replied. "Yes, sir!"

The four of us knelt at Rose's bedside as she asked Jesus into her life. While outwardly seemingly unchanged, I knew that inwardly she was in the process of being transformed.

A few days later, Rose informed me that she would voluntarily agree to be transferred to the State Hospital. I assured her that she would not be left alone there; I would make sure that someone would be by to visit her every day. I then telephoned a group of several loving Christian women in a nearby community and asked if they would be willing to visit Rose upon her arrival at the hospital. Not only were the women agreeable to this, they said that they would make certain that someone would visit Rose every day until her release.

Faithful to their promise, the women spent hours with Rose. In addition to teaching Rose how to pray and study the Bible, they taught her how to dress, act, and speak in a more socially acceptable manner. In an act of immeasurable kindness, they took it upon themselves to obtain Rose's little boy from the foster home where he had been placed by the welfare department, made provisions for an operation which corrected his birth defect, cared for him during his hospitalization and recovery, and taught Rose how to care for him as well. Even the women's husbands got involved, taking Rose's dilapidated car and totally rebuilding it.

After six weeks in the State Hospital, Rose was released. Not only did she leave with a new car, but with a new outlook toward her life and future, and with a new identity as a Christian woman.

After living for a time with the family of one of the women who had cared for her in the hospital, Rose and her son moved to a nearby state where she obtained a good job and enrolled in nursing school. (With the help and encouragement of her new friends, she had passed a high school equivalency test.) Since then, Rose has suffered neither depression nor suicidal tendencies. She has never had to see another psychiatrist.

* * *

One need not look very far to discover that there are many battered and bruised people in the world who, as a result of their unfortunate life experiences, have never learned to behave in a manner that is socially acceptable. While healing for such individuals may begin behind the walls of a hospital or doctor's office, it is essential that such individuals be further cared for by a loving, concerned, support community if their healing is to last and if they are to ultimately become accepted, productive members of society.

It would be naïveté of the worst kind, for example, to assume that a person like Rose—simply because she had been healed of her depression, or simply because she had become a Christian—would thereby be automatically transformed in all other maladjusted areas of her personality and behavior. After all, if for all your life you had been forced to think and relate to others solely in sexual terms in order to survive—or if, for all your life, no one had ever cared how you dressed, ate, walked, or talked—you would obviously be in dire need of basic instruction and guidance before reentering society's mainstream. Not only does it take specific teaching to help a person reach this point, it takes time and inordinate amounts of compassion and patience on the part of the teacher.

While there exist today numerous civic and governmental agencies whose sole purpose is to assist individuals like Rose to reenter society, it is my observation that few groups can do this job better than an active, caring Christian community. Perhaps this is because of the unique way in which the indwelling Holy Spirit empowers believers to *love*.

As I have emphasized earlier, to love in the Christian sense means to put another's well-being before your own. It is this kind of *agape*, or divine love, that inspires in believers an actual desire to serve others, for in serving others the believer is, in fact, serving the Lord. In the words of Jesus:

> "'I tell you, whenever you did this [this referring to acts of kindness such as clothing the naked, feeding the hungry, visiting the imprisoned and sick, and so on] for one of the least important of these brothers of mine, you did it for me!'" (Matt. 25:40).

At the same time, it is important to understand that agape love is not something a person can manufacture or drum up on his own. It is a gift from God, generated in the believer through God's indwelling Holy Spirit. I know that in my own life I've discovered a new capacity to love—a new quality of compassion and patience—that I simply did not possess before I became a Christian, and it is something I cannot attribute to my natural personality. The collective effect of this kind of love—as demonstrated by the caring Christian women who reached out to help Rose—is remarkable, indeed.

3

LOUISA

The Healing Power of the Eucharist

"Where, Death, is your victory? Where, Death, is your power to hurt?" . . . Thanks be to God who gives us the victory through our Lord Jesus Christ! (1 Cor. 15:55–57).

Walking down the hospital corridor, I was filled with apprehension about the new patient I was about to meet.

Louisa had just arrived at our hospital from an out-of-state institution where she had been committed for the past several months after a suicide attempt.

Louisa was the mother of five children. According to her records, her depression seemed connected to the tragic suicide of her sixteen-year-old son two years earlier. Because of her son's death, she was consumed by guilt; she accepted all blame for the death and could not forgive herself for whatever she might or might not have been able to do to prevent it. I knew how powerful a barrier unresolved grief and accompanying guilt could be against healing. As I rounded the corner and approached Louisa's door, I honestly didn't know if I would be able to help her.

"Louisa?"

Surrounded by a mountain of luggage and busily unpacking, the woman jumped, startled by my presence. She was tall and slender, with thick silver hair and gray eyes that filled with tears when I introduced myself.

"Why are you crying?" I asked.

But Louisa, overcome with emotion, only shook her head.

"Why don't you stop unpacking?" I suggested. I gestured toward the bed. "Sit down. Make yourself comfortable. Let's talk about what's bothering you."

To my dismay, Louisa began to sob uncontrollably. Several minutes passed before she regained her composure.

"Do you want me to start at the beginning?" she asked.

I nodded.

"Well," she began, "when I was a young woman I began to experience frequent periods of mild depression, but they didn't get too serious until about ten years ago. At that time I became severely depressed and irritable. I was at my worst when I was with my family, so I decided to see a psychiatrist. After a few visits, I couldn't notice any improvement, so I stopped going."

"What happened after that?"

"I went on with life, but I stopped living. That is, I just existed. My husband was a workaholic—he was always busy working late or traveling or reading—and never available when I needed him. It seemed I was always angry at him, and our relationship began to deteriorate. It got so we barely spoke to each other.

"Life went on like this until six years ago when both my aunt and father-in-law died within forty-eight hours of one another. My aunt suffered manic-depressive illness and died in a mental hospital. But the death that affected me more was my father-in-law's. I had been very close to him. He was so available, approachable, loving. I still can't believe he's gone. I mean, there's part of me that just won't believe it."

"Do you feel you ever had a chance to grieve his death?" I asked. "Do you feel that you've accepted it?"

"No," Louisa replied. "I just felt numb."

"Go on," I urged.

"Things got worse. I became more depressed, angry and hostile. Sometimes I threatened suicide. One winter night I had a terrible fight with my husband and ran out of the house into the middle of a snowstorm. I was hysterical—wandering aimlessly—and my family had to come and get me. It was then I knew I needed help, so I met with another psychiatrist in town."

"How did that work out?"

"The psychiatrist counseled me about my problems and prescribed drugs. She said I had low self-esteem. When our sessions together didn't seem to be going anywhere she began counseling my husband and me about our troubled marriage."

"With any results?"

"No. Finally, I got so desperate for relief that one afternoon I deliberately took too many pills. It wasn't that I wanted to die—although I had threatened suicide many times. I just wanted to go to sleep so I wouldn't have to face my problems. When my husband found me unconscious, he brought me to the emergency room where my stomach was pumped and I was hospitalized."

"And then?"

There was a long pause.

"Things really got bad. My father became ill and while I was out of town visiting him, my baby boy—my son, Alex—committed suicide. He was only sixteen. He sat in our car with the engine on and the garage door closed until he died of carbon monoxide poisoning.

"Of course I rushed home, but I was overwhelmed with an awful sense of meaningless and hopelessness. I couldn't even cry. Not even during the funeral. I just couldn't believe that Alex was dead. I hated myself for not being home when it happened."

"Do you feel now that you've ever really grieved and accepted your son's death?" I asked.

"No," Louisa replied. "I just feel numb."

Louisa went on to tell me of her recent suicide attempt, which had been triggered by her husband's announcement that he was seeking a divorce. He told Louisa that he no

longer loved her—he hadn't loved her for several years—
and he could no longer live with her emotional problems.

"After that," Louisa continued, "life became unbearable.
There was no sanctuary anywhere; even my own home was
a hostile place full of painful memories. Then one afternoon
I decided to end it all. I gathered up all the prescribed pills
and medications I could find and took them. Eight days
later I woke up to find that not only had I failed in my
suicide attempt, but that I had been legally committed.

"Maybe you can understand now how much I appreciate
your accepting me as a patient, Dr. Wilson. Please say you
can help me."

"I'll need to review your records more thoroughly," I
replied. "And you and I will have to spend a lot of time
together." I paused. "But if we really work hard, Louisa,
then yes, I think you can be healed."

During our next several sessions, I learned that Louisa
had grown up in a middle class home in which there was
much strife. Her father, an alcoholic, was loud and argu-
mentative and frequently unfaithful to his wife. Her mother was a cold, critical perfectionist. Though Louisa tried
desperately to meet her mother's unreasonable expectations, she most always failed and was harshly criticized. As
a result, Louisa suffered extremely low self-esteem and an
ingrained belief that she could please no one. Her sense of
inadequacy carried over into her marriage; when her workaholic husband failed to pay attention to her, she felt re-
jected and angry. It was this repeated pattern of perceived
rejection and resulting anger that was at the root of
Louisa's marital problems.

I also learned that several individuals in Louisa's family
had attempted suicide, and one aunt had actually succeeded. This was important because it is generally recognized that whenever a pattern of suicide has been established in a family, this often predisposes other family
members to consider suicide as a valid alternative to solv-
ing life's most difficult problems. Indeed, such may have

been the case not only with Louisa, but with her son as well.

Curious about Louisa's spiritual life, I asked her one afternoon what her faith meant to her.

"I'm not sure," she replied. "I can't say that I have any faith."

I discovered that Louisa's exposure to religion as a child was minimal. Her father rarely went to church, her mother only occasionally. On more careful questioning, however, I learned that Louisa had always had a sense that there was a God, and when everything went wrong, He was punishing her. Louisa's God was wrathful—one who only punished and never expressed approval—not unlike her parents. She was incapable of conceiving of a God who could love her unconditionally.

After several sessions, the cause of Louisa's resistance to treatment and deep depression became very clear. Louisa suffered depression because she had never had a chance to properly grieve and ultimately accept the death of her son and, to a much lesser extent, her father-in-law.

Grief, I should explain, is a natural process of healing which, following the death of a loved one, follows five distinct stages of resolution. These stages are: 1) numbness, or failure to accept the death of the loved one; 2) recurrent mental images of the deceased; 3) social withdrawal; 4) holding on to the attitudes and behavior of the deceased as part of one's own identity; and 5) decathexis, or final emotional detachment from the deceased. The grieving process ends and healing is complete when the survivor no longer holds on to expectations of continuing a love relationship (in a literal sense) with the deceased, and no longer views the lost loved one as a continuing recipient of his affection.

In a most tragic way, Louisa—largely because of her poor emotional health to begin with—had never progressed past the initial stage of numbness following the death of her son.

Also clear was the specific nature of Louisa's depression.

Louisa suffered a classic case of existential (or spiritual) despair of death. For Louisa, death seemed meaningless and depriving—another one of life's pointless sorrows allowed by a God that was at best punishing and at worst, indifferent. This was because Louisa had not yet developed a wholistic understanding of death from a Christian point of view.

Now that I understood the origin and specific nature of Louisa's depression, I had to discover some way to help her fully resolve her grief.

I began by suggesting to Louisa that she read the New Testament in a modern English translation in order to gain a more accurate understanding of the nature of God—particularly the unconditional quality of His love. Eager to undertake any task that might facilitate her healing, Louisa did this.

In reading the gospels, she was astounded to discover that God was neither some vague cosmic force nor a punishing ogre, but—as revealed through His incarnation in Jesus Christ—He was all-loving and forgiving. It wasn't until Louisa came across this following passage, however, that she truly began to believe that God's love and forgiveness could extend to her, too:

Dear friends, let us love one another, because love comes from God. Whoever loves is a child of God and knows God. Whoever does not love does not know God, for God is love. And God showed his love for us by sending his only Son into the world, so that we might have life through him. This is what love is: it is not that we have loved God, but that he loved us and sent his Son to be the means by which our sins are forgiven (1 John 4:7–10).

At the same time, I explained to Louisa that the bulk of her current depression stemmed from inability to properly grieve and accept the death of her son. I went on to say that sometimes, in an unhealthy way, a person holds on to an object or memory that serves to symbolize the deceased loved one.

It turned out that Louisa was, indeed, clinging to such a symbol: the green car in which her son had committed suicide. Three days after Alex's death, Louisa's husband had the car removed and destroyed. Because he had not consulted Louisa first about this, a bitter argument between the two ensued; now, the memory of the incident and of the car served as a constant reminder to Louisa of her son's death.

When Louisa and I discussed this, I asked her if she would be willing to release her bad memory of the car to God through prayer. Louisa agreed to this idea, so I suggested that while we prayed she might be open to any images that appeared in her mind's eye. This technique of imaging—or bringing forth mental pictures from the subconscious when one is in prayer or meditation—can often be instrumental in healing.

After we prayed, Louisa told me that she had seen in her mind an image of the green car driving down her driveway and out of sight. The next morning, during her devotions, she once again saw the car—this time with her son driving it off into a brilliant light. With this image, Louisa reported experiencing a great sense of release. Still, she remained depressed.

I encouraged her to remain open to the idea of imaging.

A few days later, Louisa (who was permitted to leave the hospital) was watching her nephew playing soccer at the field on the Duke campus. It was dusk and there was an ethereal golden glow over the field. Suddenly, Louisa became aware of her son's presence. Dressed in his soccer uniform, his form was diffuse, but his face was clearly discernable. Overwhelmed with the beauty of the image, Louisa watched as her son gradually diffused into the golden light and her four other children appeared. Then, she heard her son's voice say, "You have your other children who need and love you, Mom. Let me go."

Louisa's eyes welled with tears when she told me of the experience.

"It was beautiful, Dr. Wilson," she said. "But I still feel sad somehow. I don't feel that I've fully resolved my grief. I guess I still feel guilty."

It was then that I drew upon the work of my good friend and colleague, Ken McAll, a British psychiatrist who is also a Christian. The last time Ken and I had communicated, he had excitedly shared with me his discovery of the healing power of the Eucharist (also known as Holy Communion or the Lord's Supper) in completing—in a unique way—the grieving process. Through the Eucharist, Ken explained, the believer not only shares in Christ's death and resurrection, he also finds himself in mystical communion with all believers (also known as saints), including those who have died. That is, through the Eucharist the chasm between heaven and earth is bridged. In a purely spiritual sense, all believers—dead, living, and yet to be—are united as one in the body of Christ (also known as the Church).

Explaining this concept to Louisa, I suggested that she celebrate the Eucharist—at the same time offering to the Lord a prayer of commitment for Alex. By doing this, Louisa could both relinquish any remaining guilt she might have for her son's death and be given hope for his eternal happiness and wholeness in Christ.

In a quiet service in her room, Louisa did this.

When I met with her the next day, she seemed to be a different woman. Her eyes, once so sad, now sparkled with life and enthusiasm. Her speech and movements were animated and happy.

"Dr. Wilson," she said, "I can't begin to tell you how wonderful I feel. When I ate the bread and drank from the goblet, I felt the most incredible sense of release—as though I were literally surrendering all my painful memories of Alex to the Lord. At the same time, I was filled with a certain knowledge that he was still as much alive and whole and loved by Jesus up in heaven as I am down here on earth." She paused, then added, "I don't feel guilty anymore. I really believe God loves me."

Today, Louisa is healed. Although her divorce from her husband seems certain, she has begun reestablishing relationships with her children and is living a productive life. No longer is she plagued by depression. Through the healing power of the Eucharist, she found forgiveness and freedom.

"Where, Death, is your victory? Where, Death, is your power to hurt?" . . . Thanks be to God who gives us the victory through our Lord Jesus Christ! (1 Cor. 15:55–57).

Louisa has, as the scripture promises, experienced victo-'y over the sting of death through faith in Christ.

* * *

Many volumes have been written about the symbolic and experiential meaning of the Eucharist, and it is not my intention here to fully try to explain an event which the world's greatest theologians still categorize as truly mystical.

But speaking as a physician who deals on a daily basis with people who are suffering depression, despair, and utter desolation because of the loss of a loved one, I am particularly acquainted with the unique way in which the Eucharist can help a person better understand and accept death.

As so beautifully illustrated in Louisa's story, death for the Christian does not terminate the relationship between the survivor and the deceased; rather, it establishes a new potential dimension of relationship that is holy, eternal, and purely spiritual. It is through the body of Christ in the Eucharistic act that this "communion of saints" is celebrated and experienced. For the believer, therefore, death is not a loss, but a gain; not an end, but a beginning. To commune through the Eucharistic act with loved ones who have passed on before is, according to my friend Ken McAll, not only a helpful but an essential activity—one which he calls "ritual mourning" when done on a regular, continuing basis.

In addition to helping the believer through the grieving process, the Eucharist is also valuable in the way it allows a person to both symbolically and literally share in the death of Christ. In eating the bread (Christ's body) and drinking the wine (Christ's blood), the believer symbolically shares—as Jesus instructed His followers to do—in His death. In one of the earliest references to the Eucharistic tradition, Paul writes:

> For I received from the Lord the teaching that I passed on to you: that the Lord Jesus, on the night he was betrayed, took a piece of bread, gave thanks to God, broke it, and said, "This is my body, which is for you. Do this in memory of me." In the same way, after the supper, he took the cup and said, "This cup is God's new covenant, sealed with my blood. Whenever you drink it, do so in memory of me."
>
> This means that every time you eat this bread and drink from this cup you proclaim the Lord's death . . . (1 Cor. 11:23–26).

If the believer shares in Christ's death, it stands to reason that he also shares in His resurrection. And if he shares in Christ's resurrection, he also is renewed, cleansed, and empowered with His Holy Spirit. In this sense, the Eucharist, when partaken on a regular basis, can serve as a literal spiritual tonic. It is through the Eucharistic act that many healings either take place or are affirmed.

4

MICHAEL

The Healing Power of Repentance, Confession, and Forgiveness

For it is by our faith that we are put right with God; it is by our confession that we are saved. The scripture says, "Whoever believes in him will not be disappointed." This includes everyone, because there is no difference between Jews and Gentiles; God is the same Lord of all and richly blesses all who call to him. As the scripture says, "Everyone who calls out to the Lord for help will be saved" (Rom. 10:10–13).

"Michael!" I exclaimed, surprised to find my friend waiting outside my office as I arrived at work early one morning. I was alarmed at his expression—panicked, nervous, distraught. "What is it?" I asked. "Please come in. Sit down."

Michael was a handsome man, in his late fifties, with thick silver hair and the looks of an aging matinée idol. Usually Michael was a dapper dresser, but on this particular morning his rumpled clothes looked as though they had been slept in.

"Bill," said Michael, perched nervously on the edge of his chair, "you've got to help me. I've been up all night. I can't sleep. For the past several weeks I've been wanting to talk to you, but I haven't had the courage. You know me better than anyone, Bill. That's why it's so hard for me to say what I've got to say."

"Michael," I said, reaching over to place a reassuring hand on his shoulder, "I'm your friend. Nothing you say could ever change that."

Michael remained silent. For a moment I thought he was going to get up and leave. Then, in a low voice, he confessed what had been troubling him.

"You know about my homosexual past," he said. "You're the only one who knows. I've never told my wife. I've never wanted her or the kids to know about it. When I gave up that kind of life nearly twenty years ago, I was sure I'd never return to it. I was sure that God would help me. But Bill . . . Bill . . ." Michael's voice broke, and his deep-set eyes filled with tears. "I'm into it all over again, Bill. God knows I don't want to be, but I am."

"How did this happen?" I asked, trying not to show the pain that I was feeling for my friend.

"It was at a sales convention," he replied. "A trade show out west, a few months ago. I was attending a cocktail party hosted by our firm and this guy looked at me in that unmistakable way, made a few suggestive remarks, and for some reason I weakened and agreed to meet him later in his room. Since then, I've been with many men. I'm into it deeper than ever. God, Bill, what will I do? I feel so helpless. And so guilty! I know what I'm doing is so wrong. Not only am I betraying my wife and kids—I've never felt so separated from God in my life. Please don't condemn me, Bill. The main reason I've put off talking to you is because I've been so afraid that you might condemn me."

"You know me better than that," I replied. "I'm glad that you finally decided to talk to me. You're under a lot of stress now, Michael. We're going to have to sit down, put our heads together, and figure out how to get you out of this mess. We've done it before. We can do it again."

As I spoke, I was glad to see Michael relax; he settled back in his chair and seemed to breathe more easily.

I'd first met Michael several years earlier—before I was a Christian and before my practice included any consideration of my patients' religious beliefs. Michael had come under my care when he attempted suicide by an overdose of sleeping pills. When I examined him at that time, there was no reason for me to suspect his homosexual history; he was a married man with four children, actively involved in his church and community. Because of his severe depression and strong suicidal tendency, he needed to be treated immediately. Since there were in those days no antidepressant drugs available, I treated him with electric shock therapy.

At first it seemed that Michael quickly recovered. His suicidal tendency and symptoms of depression—insomnia, loss of appetite and uncontrollable crying—disappeared. I discharged him from the hospital.

In less than a month, however, I had to readmit Michael when his symptoms reappeared. Again, I treated him with electric shock therapy. During his convalescence, I began to suspect that there was something bothering Michael that he had failed to tell me.

When I first confronted Michael, he denied that there were any major areas of conflict in his life. Still not convinced, I continued to confront him. Finally, with great anguish and difficulty, he told me the following story.

Michael was born in a small mill town into a home that was, to say the least, chaotic. His father was an alcoholic— a man given to drunken rages wherein he would physically abuse both his wife and child, and who eventually deserted his family. Michael's mother, on the other hand, was a very pious Christian—an ultra-religious woman, regarded as one of the pillars of the community, but who also (perhaps because of the severe flaws in her husband) fostered a too intimate and suffocating relationship with her son.

Before Michael reached puberty, an older male cousin persuaded him to perform homosexual acts with him. In time, Michael, his cousin, and several other cousins and neighborhood kids were involved in many different kinds of homosexual and heterosexual activities. With the intense changes in sexual drive and orientation that come with puberty, Michael eventually became what is known as a polymorphously perverse homosexual. Such a person engages in all manner of perverse sexual activities as varied and bizarre as the human mind is capable of conceiving.

With the onset of World War II, Michael was drafted from high school into military service. After completing boot training, he was transferred to a unit that happened to include thirty-five homosexuals. As soon as the men had discovered each other, they initiated a series of orgies in which they performed, en masse, any sexual acts that they had either heard about or had experienced first-hand. It was only a matter of time before they were found out. One night, during one of their orgies, the men were raided by the S. P.s and arrested. Everyone was court-martialed and dishonorably discharged from the service.

Once home, Michael decided to go to college. He learned from friends about a nearby university where it was rumored that more than 50 percent of the students were homosexual. Michael enrolled. The rumor proved to be true, and soon he was involved in his usual homosexual pursuits. At the same time, he excelled in his studies and looked forward to graduating.

It was during his second year of graduate school that Michael became involved with what is known in homosexual circles as a "queen," or highly effeminate male homosexual. While Michael was well acquainted with queens in general, in the course of this particular relationship he was introduced to a homosexual act that was shocking, even to an unusually experienced person like himself. One night, while in the midst of performing this act, Michael suddenly found himself paralyzed with feelings of self-loathing, remorse, shame, and—for some strange reason—fear. From out of nowhere he suddenly realized the utter depravity of his behavior. Michael was in trouble—big trouble—and he knew it. Still, he recalled his mother's firm belief that God would save a person—no matter how lost or degenerate that person might be—if only he would call out to his Maker in time of need.

"Lord, save me!" he cried out loud.

And, as Michael explained it to me, that's just what God did.

Literally sickened by his behavior, Michael quickly pulled on his clothes, went out into the hall, and was ill. He never returned to say good-bye to his partner. From that night on, he avoided all contact with homosexuals in general. For all intents and purposes, it could be said that as a result of what happened that evening, Michael was no longer a homosexual. Through conversion, he had been instantaneously healed.

Even as a nonbeliever, I had been impressed by Michael's story. This is because homosexuality, due to the immediate pleasure and gratification it offers a person, is an extremely difficult disorder to cure.

In time, Michael graduated from college, moved to another part of the country, and obtained a good job. He married, and became the father of four handsome sons. Because of his sincere gratitude and love for the Lord, he naturally rose to a leadership position in his church. He was, in fact, looked up to by many as a model Christian. It wasn't that Michael sought this kind of adulation; his great love for the Lord was in direct response to the degree which he felt he had been forgiven. His deep humility was genuine. To be admired by others only made him feel uncomfortable.

Understanding this about Michael, it was easy to see how the next event to transpire in his life would be enough to send him into a depression so severe that it would cause him to want to take his life.

Though Michael's alcoholic father had deserted his family when Michael was very young, many family members had kept in touch with the man. One day, Michael received a telephone call from one of his siblings who informed him that his father was gravely ill and was not expected to live. After giving the matter much thought, Michael decided that although his father had done nothing but beat and berate him as a child, it was still somehow his moral duty to at least go visit the man on his deathbed.

He was stopped from going, however, by the fact that when he had left his hometown for the military service and college, many people—at least his cousins and several of the kids he had grown up with—had been well aware of his homosexuality. Michael had never told his wife about his past and never intended to. The thought of her finding out about it terrified him. What if, as he walked down his hometown street, someone were to publicly ridicule him? Or worse, what if someone were to take his wife aside and whisper some nasty comment in her ear?

The closer to death that Michael's father came, the more Michael's fears intensified. At some point he was going to have to return home—if only for his father's funeral. What was he going to do? He couldn't tell his wife that the reason he was avoiding his father was because he held a grudge against the man; such a vindictive attitude was entirely against his nature. Finally, in desperation over his dilemma, Michael took an overdose of sleeping pills. It was then that he became my patient.

While I was at that time unable to offer Michael specifically Christian counseling, God did grant me a good common-sense solution to his problem. When Michael asked me what he should do about visiting his dying father, I suggested that when the time came for him to go, he should simply get in his car with his wife and children and drive directly to the hospital. After visiting with his father, he was not to tarry, but to proceed immediately home.

Michael did this and with great success. No one taunted or teased either him or any members of his family. Indeed, it seemed that everyone he encountered had forgotten about his past. Later, when Michael's father died, he repeated, with equal success, the same procedure for attending the funeral. At last Michael's deepest fears had been put to rest. God, it would seem, had protected him.

Until now.

As I looked at Michael's tormented face, and as I considered what he had just told me about his seemingly helpless return to homosexual activities, my brow furrowed with concern. This was because I realized that the therapy that Michael and I were about to begin would not be easy, nor would it be guaranteed successful.

Homosexuality, as I have mentioned, is very hard to cure. It is interesting to note that although some psychiatrists have taken the attitude that homosexuality is not a disease, they still write about its "treatment." In one of the standard textbooks of psychiatry, J. Marmor writes that although homosexuals may present themselves for psychiatric treatment for difficulty in attracting partners, break-up of homosexual relationships, problems in self-realization, various neuroses, and depression, most of them simply want symptom relief from these specific problems. There are, however, other homosexuals—people like Michael—who seek psychiatric treatment because they are unhappy with their sexual orientation, and desire to function as heterosexuals.

Basically, homosexuality can be defined as a disease wherein a person possesses an aberrant sexual object choice. There are two schools of thought regarding the cause of homosexuality: 1) that it is partly biologically or genetically determined, which implies that the homosexual individual cannot help himself, and 2) that it is a learned behavior, largely resulting from psychological conflicts in early life. Scientific evidence overwhelmingly supports the latter theory; that is, an individual's sexual object choice is not determined biologically, but is learned.

Much has been said and published about the so-called "Christian" view of homosexuality. After much research into this issue, it is my understanding that *homosexual behavior on the part of a believer is, at best, behavior that is in direct contradiction to the tenets of the faith.* This is especially true in light of the biblical admonition found in

Paul's letter to the Romans:

> [Because those people] worship and serve what God has cre-
> ated instead of the Creator himself. . . . Because those people
> refuse to keep in mind the true knowledge about God, he has
> given them over to corrupted minds, so that they do the things
> that they should not do (Rom. 1:25–28).

For the Christian, however, there is a viable option to a
homosexual lifestyle—a conscious choice or decision that
can be made. Those "corrupt minds" can be changed. As
Paul goes on to say:

> Do not conform yourselves to the standards of this world, but
> let God transform you inwardly by a complete change of your
> mind. Then you will be able to know the will of God—what is
> good and is pleasing to him and is perfect (Rom. 12:2).

Homosexuality then, from a biblical view, would seem to
not be biologically determined, but a learned behavior pattern. It is my observation that homosexuality—like many
learned maladaptive behavior patterns such as alcoholism
and eating disorders—is controllable and changeable. For
the Christian, such maladaptive behavior patterns also in-
dicate spiritual disease; in the case of homosexuality, the
disease is manifested as a functional disturbance of sexual
desire and object choice.

Whether or not the patient is Christian, homosexuality
remains very difficult to cure. According to Marmor, successful treatment brings satisfactory changes in object
choice in only 20 to 50 percent of patients treated. Prognosis is good in 1) young persons, 2) persons with previous
heterosexual experience, 3) persons with recency of onset
of homosexual activity, and 4) persons with aggressive personality patterns. Prognosis is especially poor for homosexuals who are passive and effeminate.

In Christian literature there are numerous instances of
homosexual healings as a result of conversion. In addition

to Michael's initial experience, I have known several such cases. That there are thousands of others is a certainty, but they are rarely disclosed.

Christian faith in itself is therapeutic for the homosexual seeking healing in that it can serve to either instantaneously reorient the person, or serve as a motivating force to bring about gradual change. In Michael's case, however, simple saving faith was not enough for a lasting healing. More therapy—intensive and long-term—would be necessary.

As I explained all this to Michael, he nodded in silent agreement. Understanding fully the energy and commitment that would be required of him, he said that he would be willing to undergo intensive psychotherapy. Because of his Christian faith he was highly motivated to obtain full and permanent healing.

We began by methodically going back and considering the many traumas of Michael's childhood—the emotional and physical abuse he suffered from his father, the suffocating relationship he endured with his mother, his first and subsequent homosexual experiences he had engaged in with his cousin and other friends. Through reliving these experiences, Michael came to a much better understanding of the lack of stability in his parents' marriage and how that distorted his understanding of heterosexual love; his lack of lovingly employed discipline and how that negatively affected his sense of self-worth; his lack of a strong male role model due to his father's alcoholism and desertion; and his lack of a strong value system and consistent religious instruction due to the wildly differing nature of his parents' value systems and religious beliefs—a controlling, ultra-religious mother, and an out-of-control, irreligious father.

With this fuller understanding of the damaging effect of his early childhood, Michael was able to recognize how necessary it was for him to *acknowledge, yet leave behind his past*—to finally grow up, as it were, irregardless of the damage that had been inflicted upon him by his parents and early playmates. No longer could Michael retreat through homosexual behavior to his "little boy world" where his sexual and emotional growth had been so tragically arrested and distorted.

At the same time, I probed more deeply into the nature of Michael's spiritual life; that is, his conversion and subsequent Christian experience. In an attempt to ascertain the effect that Michael's faith could have regarding the healing of his homosexuality, I explained to him the importance of the following five key issues, and asked him these questions:

1. *Repentance:* Was Michael truly repentant about his homosexual behavior?

"Jesus saw him lying there, and he knew that the man had been sick for such a long time; so he asked him, 'Do you want to get well?'" (John 5:6).

2. *Transformation:* Did Michael really want to be transformed?

"Do not conform yourselves to the standards of this world, but let God transform you inwardly by a complete change of your mind" (Rom. 12:2).

3. *Faith:* Did Michael really expect God to change him?

"'. . .Everything is possible for the person who has faith'" (Mark 9:23).

4. *Prayer:* Was Michael willing to pray fervently for his healing?

"Is anyone among you in trouble? He should pray. . . . This prayer made in faith will heal the sick person; the Lord will restore him to health, and the sins he has committed will be forgiven. So then, confess your sins to one another and pray for one another, so that you will be healed" (James 5:13, 15–16).

5. *Will:* Did Michael really desire, above all else, God's will for his life—even if this included giving up all homosexual activities?

"'Father,' he said, 'if you will, take this cup of suffering away from me. Not my will, however, but your will be done'" (Luke 22:42).

Michael's response to all these questions was strongly affirmative—an encouraging sign.

Finally, with the aim of fully healing Michael of all his hurtful life experiences and memories, I employed the arduous and often painful three-step process of *repentance*, *confession*, and *forgiveness*.

Through *repentance*, Michael had to recognize his own responsibility in becoming the person he was; that is, he had to acknowledge his sinfulness as his *own*—not the fault or responsibility of someone else. In repenting, Michael also had to be truly sorry for the wrongness of his behavior, and he had to truly want to change. To a certain extent, the integrity of Michael's repentance was something that could only truly be known between him and God. As far as I could ascertain, however, it did seem that Michael had a repentant heart.

Once Michael had acknowledged and repented of his sins, he then *confessed* them. He confessed to me as many of his sins—for the most part, his long history of homosexual encounters—as he could remember. Sometimes it was all I could do to sit and listen to Michael's recollections, so tormented and anguished was he by their remembrance. In addition, Michael confessed the sins of his parents; that is, he confessed the deep anger, bitter resentment, and out-and-out hatred he felt toward them for the many ways they had abused him as a child.

Finally, through prayer, Michael asked God to *forgive* him for his sins, and to touch all those hurtful, empty spots in his heart with His healing love. Which God did.

It was through this process that Michael was healed. He has not, since receiving intensive Christian psychotherapy, returned to homosexual activity. He remains deeply convicted and at peace with the belief that he never will.

* * *

The three-step procedure of *repentance*, *confession*, and *forgiveness* is one of the most powerful tools that the Christian therapist has to effect change and healing. The key to this method's success is the manner in which it serves to restore a right relationship between the patient and God.

As illustrated in Michael's story, the classic motivation for repentance is emotional suffering. Suffering is an inevitable part of the human experience and a natural consequence of humankind's fallen (or sinful) nature. It is best described as an unremitting emotional state that arises as the result of some internal or external stimulus (in many cases, sinful thoughts or behavior) that elicits painful feelings such as sorrow, fear, confusion, anger, emptiness, guilt, shame, and so on. If the suffering is the type of anguish that arises from sinful thoughts or behavior, it is pain that is a direct consequence of the person's separation from God. This type of suffering can only be relieved when the person and God are reconciled.

If one is to understand the need for repentance, it is necessary to recognize the reality and nature of sin. Sin is always committed against God. Jesus made this clear when He recalled the prodigal son's confession to his father: "'I have sinned against heaven [God] and before you'" (Luke 15:21, RSV). And David, in Psalm 51, wrote: "I have sinned against you [God]—only against you—" (Ps. 51:4). Sinful behavior, therefore, whether it involves only the individual or others as well, is sin against God, and as such requires repentance that must be addressed directly to God.

It should also be noted that true repentance, or remorse for one's sin, is an attitude that can only be brought about by the Holy Spirit. It is the Holy Spirit that prompts a person to realize that one day he will have to meet God face-to-face and be judged. The topic of God's judgment is not a very popular one in this day and age, but it is, nonetheless, a topic about which Jesus frequently and adamantly spoke. A person's acceptance of his eventual judgment often causes him to experience a painful awareness of the inadequacy of self, which in turn motivates his humble appeal to God for relief. This appeal to God—through the act of repentance with a "broken and contrite heart" (Ps. 51:17, RSV)—is a profound moment when a person experiences a literal psychological change in personality. For the unregenerate person who is experiencing this kind of repentance for the first time, it is no less than his moment of conversion. For the person who already is a believer (as was the case with Michael), it is the moment of change which results in more holy (or whole) thoughts and behavior.

With repentance, a person experiences the desire to confess—first to God, and when appropriate, to certain others. In James we read: "So, then, confess your sins to one another and pray for one another, so that you will be healed" (James 5:16).

Psychologist Louis Monden has observed that "confessing one's guilt is an archetypal experience, one so deeply enclosed in the very structure of the human psyche that the need for it will never disappear." Again, I stress that while the act of confessing one's sin to a fellow believer with the intent of enlisting that person's prayers can be very helpful, to confess one's sin to another who, as a result, would be in any way offended or hurt is to be avoided at all costs. For healing to take place, it is always essential, however, for the individual to confess his sin to God.

Once a person has confessed his sin to God, there will follow this response by the One who loves unconditionally and is infinitely merciful: He forgives!

Upon receiving God's forgiveness, a person is made whole; he can accept himself because he is accepted by God; he can go on to forgive others because he is forgiven by God. Through God's forgiveness, a person is saved not only from death and slavery to sin, but also from the crippling fear of future slavery to sin. Through God's forgiveness a person is, quite literally, set free.

But, as Michael's story so effectively illustrates, even though a person is Christian, he still has coexisting with his new Holy Spirit, his old human nature. If the believer is not vigilant—and sometimes even when he is—he will experience lapses in both thought and behavior. At times, the believer will inevitably try to control his own life, and in his desire to be "free" from God's guiding influence, go on his own misguided way. When this happens (as happened to Michael when he returned to homosexual behavior) the believer quenches or grieves the Holy Spirit, and once again finds himself separated from God.

Do not quench the spirit . . . (1 Thess. 5:19, RSV).

And do not grieve the Holy Spirit of God . . . (Eph. 4:30, RSV).

This separation from God is immediately experienced as a sense of loss and emotional pain. Such negative feelings are actually initiated by the Holy Spirit, as He tries to lead the person to feel remorse for this wayward, unsurrendered part of his life.

In most cases, sinful behavior is eventually followed by the three-step procedure of repentance, confession, and forgiveness; then a right relationship between the believer and God is restored. Emotional pain and suffering is no longer a problem. The person is healed.

5

EILEEN

The Centrality of Christ
as It Relates to Healing

One Sabbath Jesus was teaching in a synagogue. A woman there had an evil spirit that had kept her sick for eighteen years; she was bent over and could not straighten up at all. When Jesus saw her, he called out to her, "Woman, you are free from your sickness!" He placed his hands on her, and at once she straightened herself up and praised God" (Luke 13:10–13).

Button-nosed and petite, Eileen reminded me for all the world of a little speckled bird dog pup. Flashing in her dark brown eyes, however, was anger as venomous as that of a deadly snake.

"I will *not* be moved to the psychiatric ward!" she hissed. "And as far as I'm concerned, you can leave my room this minute!"

Her movements were agitated as she laboriously tried to assume a more comfortable position on her hospital bed.

"How dare you imply that I'm not physically sick?" she demanded. "You've seen me walk. Surely, if you're any kind of doctor, you can perceive the pain I'm in." Her eyes narrowed to fiery slits. "I tell you I've got multiple sclerosis, and by God, I'm going to get treatment for it—whether it's here at this hospital, or somewhere else!"

I had just finished examining Eileen at the request of a neurosurgical colleague who had been unable to find in her any evidence of multiple sclerosis—or any other neurological disease.

Eileen, thirty years old and in her second marriage, was the mother of one preschool-age daughter from her former marriage, and was part-time stepmother to an older boy from her husband's previous marriage. In addition, she was employed on a full-time basis as a teacher of mentally retarded children.

Her symptoms had first appeared about nine months earlier when, following a severe cold, she had complained to her doctor of increasing depression, poor memory, dizziness, stomach and low back pains, and difficulty in understanding and concentration. Six months had passed, when Eileen learned that her cousin—a woman she had known since childhood—had developed multiple sclerosis. Because at least some of her cousin's symptoms appeared similar to her own, Eileen became increasingly convinced that this was her problem, too. In time, she assumed a bent over posture that nearly prevented her from walking.

After several unsuccessful trips to various medical centers, Eileen had been sent to our hospital for a final evaluation. In my examination of her, I—like my neurosurgical colleague—had been unable to find any evidence of neurological disease. I had, however, found much evidence that Eileen was suffering from severe depression with hypochondriacal symptoms—primarily her peculiar bent over posture and gait. I realized from the start that Eileen would probably not be pleased with my observation that her problems were psychologically, not biologically, determined—or with my suggestion that she be transferred to the psychiatric service for treatment. Her angry response, therefore, had not surprised me.

"I'm sorry that you're angry with the results of my examination," I said. "But as a physician and as a Christian, it's the best I have to offer."

For a moment I stopped, surprised that I had involuntarily mentioned my Christianity. This was a most unusual thing for me to do at a first meeting with a patient—not only as a matter of general policy, but because at that time I had only just begun integrating my faith with my work. Dismissing the slip as a minor indiscretion, I started to walk toward the door.

"Good day, Eileen," I said. "Since you will not agree to be transferred to the psychiatric service, I will inform your doctor that you do not desire further treatment and that you are ready to return home."

"Wait!" cried Eileen. "Come back!"

I stopped, turning to regard her quizzically.

"I'll go," she said softly.

"Well, now," I commented. "That's a switch. What caused you to change your mind?"

"Never mind that," said Eileen. "Just go ahead and make arrangements for my transfer." She hesitated. "You will be my doctor, won't you?"

"That's right," I replied. "I'll be your doctor."

"Good," said Eileen, more to herself than to me. "That's all I needed to know." With apparent difficulty, she lowered her head onto her pillow and closed her eyes.

Once Eileen was settled in the psychiatric ward, we began daily one-hour sessions through which I made every effort to unravel her past in order to gain a better understanding of the origins of her illness.

Raised in a middle-class home, and with much love and affection, Eileen's early life was reasonably tranquil. It was during her years at a state university, however, that the going began to get rough.

Before graduating, Eileen decided to marry. Shortly thereafter, she became pregnant and dropped out of school. Before her child was born, Eileen realized that her relationship with her husband was fast deteriorating. Shortly after her daughter's birth, Eileen—confused and frightened—separated from her husband and obtained a divorce. For Eileen, a girl who had not experienced too much conflict in her early life, the effect of the breakup of her first marriage was devastating. Because she had always assumed that she would marry, have a family, and live happily ever after, it was especially hard for her not to view her divorce as a personal failure.

Eventually, Eileen returned to college where she obtained a degree in special education and began her work with mentally retarded children. She also married for a second time; but from the start this marriage, too, was in big trouble. Eileen's second husband, Rick, had an unhealthy emotional dependency on his parents, who lived just a block away and who were constantly interfering with their son's and daughter-in-law's lives. He also had a continuing bad relationship with his ex-wife, a woman who unfortunately chose to use their son as a weapon in their never-ending battles. For Eileen, a sensitive person, such goings-on were a continual source of anxiety and stress. The highly emotional and often frustrating nature of her work with retarded children didn't serve to help matters any.

Because she had already been through one divorce, the thought of going through such a debilitating experience a second time was too much for Eileen to bear. As a result, she became severely depressed.

Unfortunately for her mental health, Eileen denied her depression—even to herself—and did her best to put on a happy face for her family, in-laws, friends, and co-workers. In her supreme effort to maintain her fragile self-esteem, she gradually began to transfer all her psychological and emotional problems to physical complaints. When her cousin developed multiple sclerosis, this provided Eileen with the ideal multi-symptomatic disease through which she could then focus all her unhappiness.

In psychiatry, this transference of psychological problems to physical symptoms (symptoms which are, for the patient, very real) is known as hypochondria. To Eileen's mind, at least, it was far more socially acceptable to be physically rather than mentally sick. And through being the hapless victim of multiple sclerosis, she was able to avoid facing the reality of her depression and the problems in her marriage.

While Eileen readily admitted to me that she did suffer from stress and possibly from depression, she *would not believe* that she did not actually have multiple sclerosis. Session after session we wrestled with this issue; she was particularly upset by my insistence that until she acknowledged the true origins of her symptoms, they would not go away.

In one of our early sessions, I asked Eileen if she was a Christian, explaining to her that if she really wanted to be healed, this could be of great help. She responded that she thought she was, but that she also had long desired a deeper understanding of the faith.

The more we discussed this, the more evident it became to me that although Eileen had received basic Christian instruction while growing up, her concept of Christian theology was far more God-centered than Christ-centered; because of this, she had never sought to establish a personal, Holy Spirit-empowered relationship with God *through belief in Christ*. In response to Eileen's expressed interest, I discussed this idea with her at length—stressing that in order to truly be spiritually regenerated through faith in Christ, a person must totally surrender or "put to death" his will in deference to God's will.

> And he said to them all, "If anyone wants to come with me, he must forget himself, take up his cross every day, and follow me. For whoever wants to save his own life will lose it, but whoever loses his life for my sake will save it . . ." (Luke 9:23–24).

This kind of total surrender, I explained, is a supernatural occurrence in that it is an act that goes entirely against a person's human nature. It is, however, easier to do when one understands that in surrendering, he is putting his life in the hands of a God who loves him unconditionally, who will take care of him, who will put his best interests first, and who—if permitted—will guide him on the path to wholeness.

One afternoon, little more than a week after her admittance to the hospital, Eileen prayed for Jesus to enter her life, and for the infilling of His Holy Spirit.

Still, Eileen would not believe that she did not have multiple sclerosis.

Finally, as a last resort, I asked Eileen if she would be willing to ask God to help us determine whether or not she had multiple sclerosis. She thought this was a fine idea. I asked her if she would be willing to pray that the symptoms of her actual illness—be it depression or multiple sclerosis—be magnified many times over so as to leave us no doubt. Again Eileen agreed—although when we prayed together, it was with confidence on her part that I would, in the end, be shown that she truly did suffer multiple sclerosis.

What happened next surprised even me.

For the next three days, as if in direct response to our prayer, Eileen's depression was greatly magnified. During this time, Eileen cried continuously and was so depressed she could barely lift her head from the pillow. Finally, she summoned me.

"Dr. Wilson," she sobbed, "you were right. I don't have multiple sclerosis. I'm depressed. Terribly, terribly depressed. I can't stand feeling this way much longer. Please, what can I do to be healed?" She regarded me with tear-filled eyes.

"Let's pray again," I suggested. "Let's pray for God to relieve both your depression and your bent over condition."

In two days, Eileen was walking normally.

Four weeks later, after intensive therapy through which Eileen gained further insight into the origins of her illness and also learned how to integrate more effectively her Christian faith into her daily life, she was well enough to go home.

On the day of Eileen's departure, I entered her room to

bid her a fond farewell. Considering the exceedingly positive and cooperative nature of our relationship, it was hard
for me to believe how hostile she had been on the day we
first met. Curious, I asked her again why she had changed
her mind and agreed to be transferred to the psychiatric
service for treatment.

For a moment Eileen grew thoughtful. Then a warm,
wonderful smile lit her face.

"When we first met, you mentioned that you were a
Christian," she replied. "You may not believe this, but
somehow I sensed that because of your faith, you were the
one person who might have the answer to my problem."

But Eileen's story does not end here.

Two weeks after her dismissal from the hospital, I received from her the following letter. It is a letter, I should
mention, which has in itself served as the catalyst for healing for at least thirty-five other patients of mine who have
read it over the past several years.

Dear Dr. Wilson,

I knew it wouldn't be easy when the time came to say good-
bye to you, but I really wasn't prepared for the emotions that
hit me at that moment of parting. It seemed as though each
step you took away from us [Eileen's husband, Rick, had come
to pick her up at the hospital] down the corridor took some of
my confidence with you. Although I said nothing, I wanted to
cry, "Stop! Wait! I'm frightened!" Panicky questions began to
flash through my mind: *Now, who will help me? Now, who can
I talk to? How am I going to feel when I get home? What will I
do?* I tried to pray, but all that came was a silent scream for
help.

It took six hours to travel from Durham to home. During the
drive, I tried to push the fear, doubt, and dread out of my
mind, hoping that my very real desire to return home to my
loved ones and resume a normal life would come forward to
comfort and calm me. Rick and I didn't talk much—and the
little bit we did seemed more of an exercise in skillful evasion.

As the distance between us and home closed in, I could no longer deny my anxiety.

We drove directly to Rick's parents' house. The first person I saw was Emily [Eileen's daughter]. She threw her little arms around me and said, "Momma, are you well? Please be well, Momma, and don't ever get sick again and leave us. Momma, you missed Christmas, and David's birthday [David is Eileen's step-son], and I lost two teeth, and Momma, I love you!" Her sweet chatter tore my heart to pieces. I was unable to speak for my feelings of guilt and regret about my illness were too intense. My father-in-law and brother-in-law both welcomed me. My mother-in-law, however, barely looked at me. We didn't stay long, but the short time we were there was spent in tense, uneasy, superficial conversation. Every effort was made by all to avoid the words "hospital" or "psychiatry." Finally, I volunteered that I felt better and that my doctor was a truly brilliant psychiatrist. I had hoped that I could, perhaps, ease the tension by saying the "no-no" words. But I didn't. It was more like dropping a large piece of lead. I could almost hear the "thump"! We left.

Home at last! But not the home I knew. Everything was clean and orderly. Too clean and orderly. There were no cups on the table, no toys on the floor. In the library, every book was in place, and all the clothes were washed and put away. It wasn't the same friendly, lived-in home I remembered. As the evening grew later, I began to feel depressed. The first time I had by myself was in my bath. Again, I tried to pray. I told God that I didn't know what was wrong and asked Him to help me find the problem causing my depression. After that my mind began to wander. I couldn't pray.

Sunday wasn't the day I had hoped for. For starters, we didn't go to church. Both of us knew that we didn't look forward to the inevitable questions that friends would ask us: "What did they find out at the hospital? Why were you gone so long?" I also began to panic about facing my teaching supervisor, so I called and asked my substitute to stay with my class just one more day. Somehow, the idea of returning to work on Tuesday instead of Monday didn't seem so frightening. Throughout the day, I noticed my symptoms were returning. I felt absolutely wretched, both in body and mind. I tried to think of God, and I tried to pray, but I only felt a peculiar nagging inside me. I was determined, however, to make it through the day. *You can do it*, I told myself. *Just take it slow and easy*. I fell asleep in agony and confusion, and hating myself for feeling so bad.

On Monday, I woke up even worse.

With every effort in me, I cooked breakfast—and I was nearly crawling from one room to the next trying to help Emily dress for school. After taking her to school, I went to the Board of Education where I asked for my contract, which needed my signature in order for me to resume teaching. I signed it quickly and went straight home.

As I walked into the house, I knew something was very wrong. That nagging, sick, horrible feeling inside me began to grow and spread. I couldn't see clearly, there was a ringing in my ears, and everything seemed all wrong. I tried to rest, but I couldn't. I tried to play the piano, but I couldn't. I tried to read, but I couldn't. Over a period of two hours I noticed every little pain, and how they grew worse and worse.

And then, something happened. I felt as though I was being forced to the floor. I didn't have the strength to resist. I began to hurt and burn and my mind was filled with confusion. All of my bent-over symptoms were back, but magnified hundreds of times! It was the most horrible thing I have *ever* experienced! The more I struggled, the worse it was. I tried to resist, I tried to fight it, I tried to move, but I couldn't. I was struggling with every bit of strength and will I had! Then, as though struck by a mighty blow, I was literally forced to my knees. It was at that moment I knew what was happening. All you had said to me about the need to totally surrender my stubborn will to Christ came back to me in a flood of memories, and I knew that I was struggling against God! My will against His!

"I give up!" I cried. "Oh, God, take my will! Take *all* my will! Please God, forgive me for my horrible human pride! I only want Your will and the ability to serve You! Please—take my will, and use me!"

I felt something like a little brushing against my shoulder and *instantly* all pain, confusion, and the ringing in my ears vanished. I felt a lifting sensation—and something else. Dr. Wilson, you may think I've flipped, but I tell you in that very instant I had knowledge that would take me hours, perhaps days to tell you. It wasn't a vision, and I didn't hear anything, but I *understood* things. I understood exactly what had been happening to me and why. I understood the roles of everyone who had been involved in my life during this past year. I understood that it wasn't I who sought God; but rather, God who sought me and who has been with me every second of every day. For each time I failed to respond to opportunities for health and wholeness that He offered me, I believe that I became more burdened with illness. I understood that I had been sent to Duke's Hospital for the specific purpose of meeting you. I was placed under your care for preparation. In the hospital I was given temporary peace in order to be shaped and molded and turned to face the right direction. For some reason, this is how God uses you. He seeks people out and sends them to you for healing. You look at them as a mess of confusion, and then start your job of sorting, placing, fitting, preparing—until the point where God takes over. And each of us sent to you is different. I could go on and on. But I hope we will meet again soon and then perhaps we can talk about this. But just let me say what you did for me. My problem stemmed from never having accepted Christ into my life, and never having submitted my will to God. You set me straight about Jesus. When I think of Him on the cross dying so that I might live, I feel so humble and grateful—and ashamed—for I'm truly not worthy of such a precious gift. It is wonderful to be so loved. You also set me straight about my stubborn will. I thought I had surrendered my will to God while in the hospital. But I found I had kept some part of it in a corner of my soul and in doing so had not been honest with either God or myself. Believe me, Dr. Wilson, I want no part of my will after what happened to me on Monday morning.

I still can't help wondering why God loves me so much. I am not special in any way. I don't know exactly what the future holds, but I feel so privileged that God wants me to be His instrument. The thought fills me with joy and anticipation.

I can almost hear your question: "How has your life changed because of all this?" Dr. Wilson, I will tell you. The first thing I noticed was I can rest peacefully. I found myself singing while I *cooked!* [Eileen had never been fond of cooking.] Now that I've been home a few days, my home seems beautiful and friendly. It seems I love my family more.

On Tuesday, I went to work with joy in my heart. My sweet students looked beautiful to me. It was wonderful to be back. In the afternoon my supervisor traveled all the way from her office downtown to visit me at the school and welcome me back. She said that while I had been away, the whole School Board had *prayed* for me!

Even the parents of my students called and came to visit. Every one of them said they had prayed for me. My teacher's aide said that the students had prayed every day for me. Even my principal put his arms around me and said, "Welcome home." Can you believe it? I really had no idea these people were praying for me. I told my supervisor about what I had experienced the day before. I was a little afraid she would think I had flipped, but she said, "Well, Eileen, you always were a good person. Still, I always wondered why you weren't so sure about Christianity."

"New Christian exuberance?"

I don't know, Dr. Wilson. I don't even want to question what it is. I just want to live day by day and dedicate my life to God each day through Jesus Christ, my Lord. There is something that God wants me to do with my life. I don't know right now exactly what it is. I may not know even as I'm in the midst of doing it! But that doesn't matter. Whatever God has planned for me will come to pass whether I'm aware of it or not. What I do know is that when it does come, He will guide me every step of the way. I am His happy servant!

I am so grateful to have known you, Dr. Wilson. I thank God every day for sending me to you. You and your family are in our prayers each day, and I look forward to the time when we will meet again.

> With love and gratitude,
> Eileen

I still hear from Eileen every now and then. Though her troubled marriage eventually did fall apart and she married a third time—also unsuccessfully—she is now happily remarried to her second husband, Rick, who has also become a Christian. While the past few years were not easy for Eileen, she handled her trials with admirable equanimity;

and her life, for the most part, has been filled with much love, joy, and peace. According to Eileen, her greatest pleasure is sharing the story of her healing to bring others to a saving and healing knowledge of Christ. Indeed, her story is one that vividly brings to mind the last line of Luke's telling of Jesus' healing of the woman who was all "bent over": "He [Jesus] placed his hands on her, and at once she straightened herself up and praised God" (Luke 13:13).

I should add that Eileen's recovery will always be of special significance to me in that it made a great impression on me early in my career as a Christian psychiatrist.

In the past, as a secular physician who worshiped science, humanism, and academic achievement, I probably would have accepted full credit for Eileen's healing. But Eileen had been different. As the result of Christ's participation in her healing, Eileen had left my care with a new dimension to her personality that others I had treated did not have—Christ's indwelling Holy Spirit. In this sense, Eileen had been more than healed. Through applied Christian psychotherapy, she had—in a most remarkable way—gone beyond recovery.

*   *   *

In order for a person to be healed through applied Christian psychotherapy, it is necessary that he or she first be reconciled to God. Typically, as illustrated in many of the case histories in this book, this is accomplished through conversion, in which a person surrenders his life to Christ and, in turn, receives His indwelling Holy Spirit. Eileen's story provides an excellent example of how even the person who has been raised in the Christian church may never have sought to establish a personal relationship with the living Christ. For whatever reason, such a person has never had the wonderful experience of knowing Jesus as his

personal friend, his loving guide, and—most importantly—
his intercessor to God. For the person who does not have
Christ as central in his life, the Christian experience is
often weak and ineffective. This is because Christ, and only
Christ, is the single key to a power-filled relationship with
God.

To commune with God in a harmonic relationship is perhaps a person's most primal need. It has been my observation and personal experience that there is no other religion,
philosophy, or person—living or dead—that bridges the
gap between God and humankind as does Christianity
through the living Christ. Theologian J. I. Packer, in his
response to the question, "Isn't one religion as good as
another?" in the book *Hard Questions*, observes:

> [The apostle Paul] sees man as having an inescapable sense
> of God which obliges him to worship something, yet as having
> an antipathy to God, induced by sin [or fallen human nature],
> which impels him not to worship the God who made him. So he
> distorts and falsifies the knowledge of God given him in gener-
> al revelation [through creation]. Hence spring the many forms
> of non-Christian religion, all containing details that are right in
> an overall setting that is wrong, and all *conspicuously lacking
> knowledge of God's forgiveness in Christ*, of which general
> revelation tells nothing (Emphasis mine).*

It was Christ Himself who made this point abundantly
clear when He explained to the disciple Thomas: "I am the
way, the truth, and the life; no one goes to the Father
except by me" (John 14:6).

It was through embracing rather than avoiding a personal relationship with Christ that Eileen became a living tes-
timonial to God's promise: "When anyone is joined to

---

*Taken from *Hard Questions* edited by Frank Colquhoun. © 1976 by The
Church Pastoral Aid Society, London, and used by permission of InterVarsity
Press, Downers Grove, IL 60515.

Christ, he is a new being; the old is gone, the new has come" (2 Cor. 5:17). Time and again I have observed that it is people who allow Christ to be central in their lives who are much more dramatically empowered to experience healing and wholeness, and—in the end—whose lives are lived out in rewarding service to the Lord.

Epilogue

There is a special reason that I selected Eileen's story to appear last in this book. It is a reason that will become clear once you have read the following letter, written to me just a few months after Eileen left my care by a friend of hers—a woman I did not know and to this day have never met.

Dear Dr. Wilson:

I know you have never heard of me, but we do have a mutual acquaintance in Eileen. You helped her, and cured her sick soul. She has told me all about her problems and what you did for her.

I had problems equally distressing. While my physical complaints did turn out to be real, they were thankfully not so dangerous as I had feared. Emotionally, however, I had reached such a depth of despair and agony—the culmination of nearly thirty years of depression—that I felt I couldn't go on anymore.

As a result, on several occasions I lost touch with reality. Within one six-week period I made two serious attempts to commit suicide. Oh, I was sick all right. I was sick clear through.

Everyone kept telling me, "You need God." But everything they said turned me off. I didn't want religion. I didn't believe in it. I didn't feel I needed it. I thought I could just go along my merry way and cure myself with the help of a psychologist.

163

Then Eileen came and visited me in the hospital. When she started to tell me her story I thought I would probably cut her off before she could finish, like I'd done with others. Well, for some reason I didn't. I listened to what Eileen had to say. With all my heart, and soul, and mind, I listened. She spent three hours with me that night.

After Eileen left, I thought about all she had told me. It was near midnight when I got down on my knees on the floor of that lonely, crummy hospital room, and asked God to take me—all of me—and do with me what He wished. I told Him that I could no longer take care of myself. I told Him that I needed Him, just as a child needs his parents. It was then that a wonderful thing happened. I felt God enter me! I felt Him take my hand and lift me to where I felt human again, clean and new—like I'd just been born!

Now, I pray constantly. I read the Bible with new eyes. My thoughts are much more positive. Whenever I am anxious or fearful, I ask God to give me reassurance and confidence. I ask Him to keep His hand wrapped tightly around mine. He answers all my prayers—no matter how small, or seemingly insignificant.

I had lost almost everything—my husband, my children, my life—until Eileen, with her story of healing through Christ, helped me to take that small, yet gigantic leap of faith.

If you hadn't helped Eileen the way you did, she couldn't have helped me. Having studied psychology in college, I know now that the two—psychology and Christianity—go hand in hand.

I recognize that I still need psychological counseling, and I may for some time to come. But I feel more peaceful, more self-confident, more whole than I ever have. I'm still basically the same person, but the Hell I carried around inside me is gone. What's more, I firmly believe it is gone for good.

Thank you, Dr. Wilson, for Eileen and for me. I pray for you and your family, and I pray that your ideas about psychiatry and Christianity will be universally accepted in your lifetime. I, for one, am convinced that it is the one sure way to wholly cure someone.

In God's hand and love,
Lauren

* * *

As so beautifully illustrated by Lauren's letter, not only does healing attained through Christian therapy enable a person to live a more effective life, it also enables him to reach out and *serve others*. To serve others is, after all, the primary goal of the Christian faith. But Christ-like selflessness can occur only when a person is wholly healed and thereby freed from the slavery of self—when a person, through the indwelling personality of Christ's Holy Spirit, actually desires and obtains pleasure from serving others.

This is what happened to Eileen. After being healed and filled with Christ's Holy Spirit, she was then inspired to reach out and offer what she knew of His healing love to Lauren.

And this, dear reader, is precisely what can happen to you, too.

Now that you have completed reading this book, it is my fondest hope that you will be able to incorporate many of the ideas expressed here into your own life, thus experiencing a new level of wholeness that you may never before have dreamed possible. It is likewise my hope that you will, in turn, be given the power—as Eileen was—to reach out and offer the healing touch of Christ's love to others.

As the many first-hand accounts in this book proclaim: God is alive! He does heal! What's more, He loves you, and it is His deepest desire that through faith in Him, your life will be immeasurably improved. He's done it for others. He'll do it for you.

All you have to do is ask.

How to Get Help

If you or someone you love is in need of professional Christian counseling, contact any of the following agencies for the name of a qualified Christian therapist in your area.

The Christian Association for Psychological
Studies, International
J. Harold Ellens, Ph.D., Executive Director
26705 Farmington Road, Farmington Hills, MI 48018
Phone: 313-477-1350, 474-0514

Christian Medical Society
P.O. Box 689
1616 Gateway Blvd.
Richardson, TX 75080
Phone: 214-783-8384

Narramore Christian Foundation
Box 5000
1409 North Walnut Grove Avenue
Rosemead, CA 91770
Phone: 818-288-7000